DO ALL
INDIANS
Live In
TIPIS?

FOREWORD BY
RICK WEST

INTRODUCTION BY
WILMA MANKILLER

Collins
An Imprint of HarperCollinsPublishers

IN ASSOCIATION WITH THE NATIONAL MUSEUM OF
THE AMERICAN INDIAN, SMITHSONIAN INSTITUTION

DO ALL
INDIANS
Live In
TIPIS?

Questions and Answers from the
NATIONAL MUSEUM
OF THE AMERICAN INDIAN

FIRST EDITION

The National Museum of the American Indian is committed to advancing knowledge and understanding of the Native cultures of the Western Hemisphere—past, present, and future—through partnership with Native people and others. The museum works to support the continuance of culture, traditional values, and transitions in contemporary Native life. The museum's publishing program seeks to augment awareness of Native American beliefs and lifeways, and educate the public about the history and significance of Native cultures.

For information about the Smithsonian's National Museum of the American Indian, visit the NMAI website at www.AmericanIndian.si.edu. To support the museum by becoming a member, call 1-800-242-NMAI (6624) or click on "Membership & Giving" on the website.

National Museum of the American Indian
Project Director: Terence Winch, Head of Publications
Editor: Sally Barrows

Designed by Janet M. Evans

Front cover (left to right): Tonto (Jay Silverheels [Mohawk]) and the Lone Ranger (Clayton Moore) hard at work in their familiar television show, ca. 1949–1957. © Bettmann/CORBIS. Santiago McKinn with Apache children, Canyon de los Embudos, Sonora, Mexico, March 1886. Photo by Cadmillus Sydney Fly. Smithsonian Institution National Anthropological Archives. SPC BAE 4605 01604807. "We're here to escape religious persecution. What are you here for?" Donald Reilly © 2003 *The New Yorker* Collection from cartoonbank.com. All rights reserved. Chief Joseph (Nez Perce, 1840–1904), wrapped in a Pendleton blanket, ca. 1901. Photo by Major Lee Moorhouse, courtesy of Pendleton Woolen Mills.

Library of Congress Cataloging-in-Publication Data

Do all Indians live in tipis? : questions and answers / from the National Museum of the American Indian. — 1st ed.
    p. cm.
  ISBN: 978-0-06-115301-3
  ISBN-10: 0-06-115301-X
  1. Indians of North America—Study and teaching.   2. Indians of North America—Public opinion.   3. Indians of North America—Social life and customs.   4. Indians in popular culture—North America.   5. Public opinion—North America.   6. Questions and answers.   7. Stereotypes (Social psychology)—North America.   I. National Museum of the American Indian (U.S.)   II. Title.

E76.6.D6 2007
970.004'97—dc22   2007060874

08   09   10   11   WBC / QW   10 9 8 7 6 5 4

The questions in this book originated for the most part in letters, emails, phone calls, and in-person visits from the public to the learning center at the George Gustav Heye Center, the New York branch of the National Museum of the American Indian.

CONTRIBUTORS FROM THE
NATIONAL MUSEUM OF THE AMERICAN INDIAN

Mary Ahenakew (Cherokee)

Stephanie Betancourt (Seneca)

Miranda Belarde-Lewis (Tlingit/Zuni)

Jennifer Erdrich, of Turtle Mountain Chippewa descent

Liz Hill (Red Lake Band of Ojibwe)

Nema Magovern (Osage)

Rico Newman (Piscataway/Conoy)

Arwen Nuttall (Cherokee)

Edwin Schupman (Muscogee)

Georgetta Stonefish Ryan (Delaware)

Tanya Thrasher (Cherokee Nation of Oklahoma)

Special thanks to Ellen Jamieson, whose long experience at the museum's learning center and extensive research into Native cultures has greatly contributed to our collective knowledge.

To Dr. Helen Maynor Scheirbeck (Lumbee),
whose lifelong commitment to creating
educational opportunities for Native people
is matched only by her dedication to educating
all Americans about Native cultures

CONTENTS

Popular Myths

Clothing, Housing, Food, and Health

Ceremony and Ritual

Sovereignty

Animals and Land

Language and Education

Love and Marriage

Art, Music, Dance, and Sports

Further Reading

Index

FOREWORD

Before I became the founding director of the National Museum of the American Indian, I was a practicing attorney, and sometimes, when I hear the odd—and even offensive—questions that almost every Indian must bear, I want to rise up and shout, "I object!" Few groups in the world have been as stereotyped as Native North Americans. From savage to Noble Savage, stoic to scalper, proto-environmentalist to casino millionaire, the image of Indians in American life has been subject to persistent mainstream distortions for five hundred years. In addition to stereotypes, a great deal of misinformation and ignorance influences most people's view of Native Americans. All of this can be disheartening to confront. I, and my Native colleagues, am sometimes tempted to tune it out. Most often, however, we try to bring to the table a sense of humor, along with optimism in the ability of people to learn and change.

The poet Diane Burns (Chemehuevi/Chippewa), who passed away while this book was in production, gets the Indian take on this situation in a searing poem called "Sure You Can Ask Me a Personal Question." Here are a few lines from the piece:

> *No, we are not extinct.*
>
> *Yeah, it was awful what you guys did to us.*
> *It's real decent of you to apologize.*
> *No, I don't know where you can get peyote.*
> *No, I don't know where you can get Navajo rugs real cheap.*
>
> *No, I didn't make it rain tonight.*
>
> *This ain't no stoic look.*
> *This is my face.*

Diane's poem erupts with the anger and frustration of having always to explain and define yourself to people with heads full of nonsense, prejudice, and clichés.

As much as I understand and identify with the voice in the poem, this book proposes a different kind of response to those never-ending questions. In *Do All Indians Live in Tipis?* a formidable lineup of Native writers, most of them drawn from the staff of the National Museum of the American Indian, brings an even-tempered and judicious poise to the answers you will discover here.

At the National Museum of the American Indian, we hold that it is only when a people assume authority over their stereotypes that they can truly begin to dispel them. Only by citing facts and stories from their own communities and tribal cultures can Native people hope to convey the breadth and richness of Native life in this hemisphere, both today and in the past. There are more than five hundred tribes in the United States alone, and tens of millions of indigenous peoples in Latin America, far too large and diverse a population for one little book to offer any kind of exhaustive treatment. But *Do All Indians Live in Tipis?* is, I think, an excellent start.

More than most of the books published by the National Museum of the American Indian, this volume has been a collaborative staff effort. Inspired by the questions put to the staff of our Resource Centers, both in the George Gustav Heye Center in New York City and at our flagship museum in Washington, D.C., the book has benefited from the indefatigable research abilities of its ten authors, the tenacity and imagination of Terence Winch, the head of our Publications Office, the editorial skills of Sally Barrows, and the generosity of our manuscript reviewers: Jose Barreiro (Taíno), Olivia Cadaval, George Cornell (Sault Ste. Marie Tribe of Chippewa of Michigan), Mary Jane Lenz, Gerald McMaster (Plains Cree and member of the Siksika Nation), Niki Sandoval (Chumash), Edwin Schupman (Muscogee), Clifford E. Trafzer, of Wyandot ancestry, and Herman J. Viola.

The questions and answers herein embrace a wide range of issues and topics, not simply the stereotypes. It is our hope that this book will serve a useful purpose in the marketplace of ideas and information: an authoritative, all-Native text on a compelling array of questions about Indians.

—W. RICHARD WEST, JR.
(Southern Cheyenne and member of the Cheyenne and Arapaho Tribes of Oklahoma)
Founding Director, National Museum of the American Indian

INTRODUCTION

The opening of the National Museum of the American Indian in the fall of 2004 represented the most significant Native American cultural event of the early twenty-first century. The museum's exhibitions, publications, and educational programs allow Native people to tell their own stories about their histories, rich cultures, and contemporary lives. It is fitting, then, that *Do All Indians Live in Tipis?*, which is grounded in the diverse experiences and research of its Native authors, is being published by the museum.

Even after hundreds of years of living in formerly Native villages, towns, and communities, many Americans know very little about the original people of this land. Our names (my own last name is a mistranslation into English), histories, reservations, governments, ceremonies, identities, and even our clothing—all are subject to a great deal of confusion and oversimplification. I think this book is the kind of effort that recognizes the power of education to profoundly alter the public perception of Native people in the Americas. For several years the contributors to *Do All Indians Live in Tipis?* went about the daunting task of collecting and synthesizing information on diverse topics, propelled by a fundamental belief in the public's willingness to learn about cultures that may be geographically near but very different from their own.

In 1963 President John F. Kennedy said, "For a subject worked and reworked so often in novels, motion pictures, and television, American Indians are the least understood and the most misunderstood of us all." Regrettably, this statement is as true today as it was more than forty years ago. Many negative stereotypes persist.

A surprising number of non-Natives apparently believe tribal people still live and dress as they did some three hundred years ago. During my tenure as principal chief of the Cherokee Nation, the onslaught of summer visitors often included crestfallen tourists who wanted to know, "Where are all the Indians?" With tongue in cheek, I would answer quite truthfully, "They are probably at Wal-Mart!"

Presented in an easy-to-navigate, question-and-answer format, *Do All Indians Live in Tipis?* is an impressive effort to address some of the most common misperceptions about Native Americans. The book will help eliminate stereotypes and misinformation created and perpetuated by a lack of accurate information about Native Americans in the schools, the media, and popular books and films. Providing detailed, factual answers to many of the most commonly asked questions about Native people, the book is an important reference for anyone interested in Native American history, government, culture, life, and issues.

—WILMA MANKILLER
Former Principal Chief,
Cherokee Nation of Oklahoma

IDENTITY

WHAT IS THE CORRECT TERMINOLOGY: AMERICAN INDIAN, INDIAN, NATIVE AMERICAN, OR NATIVE?

All of the above terms are acceptable. The consensus, however, is that whenever possible, Native people prefer to be called by their specific tribal name. Native peoples in the Western Hemisphere are best understood as thousands of distinct communities and cultures. Many Native communities have distinct languages, religious beliefs, ceremonies, and social and political systems. The inclusive word *Indian* (a name given by Christopher Columbus, mistakenly believing he had sailed to India, a term used by the Spanish to refer to much of southern Asia) says little about the diversity and independence of the cultures.

In the United States, *Native American* has been widely used but is falling out of favor with some groups, and the terms *American Indian* or *indigenous Americans* are now preferred by many Native people. *Native American*, however, grew out of 1960s and 1970s political movements and is now used in legislation. Legally, it refers not only to the indigenous people of the lower forty-eight states but also to Native people in U.S. territories. As an adjective, many people now prefer to use simply *Native* or *Indian*.

Canadians, too, have addressed the question of names—many Native Canadians, especially Métis (people of indigenous and French descent) and Inuit people, reject the appellation *Indian*. Similarly, the Inuit, Yup'ik, and Aleut peoples in Alaska see themselves as separate from Indians. Canadians have developed a range of terms, including *aboriginal*, *First Nations*, and *First Peoples*.

In Central and South America the direct translation for *Indian* has negative connotations. As a result, Spanish speakers use the word *indígenas*.

—MARY AHENAKEW

"We've thought and thought, but we're at a loss
about what to call ourselves. Any ideas?"

SHOULD I SAY *TRIBE* OR *NATION*?

Tribe, nation, community, pueblo, *rancheria*, village, band— American Indian people describe their own cultures and the places they come from in many ways. Often, the words *tribe* and *nation* are used interchangeably, but for many Native people they can hold very different meanings. Each community has a word or phrase in its own language that identifies it, as well as an official name recognized by the federal or state government. When being introduced to a Native person, it is appropriate to ask what community the person comes from and how he or she likes to be described. For example, many members of the Navajo Nation of Arizona (the largest tribe in the country) refer to themselves as Diné, the Navajo word meaning "the people." In this instance, you would refer to a Navajo person as being Diné, or a member of the Navajo Nation. Similarly, members of the Comanche Nation of Oklahoma refer to themselves as Nųmųnųu, which also translates to "the people."

Although many tribal groups are known by official names that include the word *nation*, like the Navajo Nation or the Comanche Nation, typically the U.S. government uses the word *tribe* when referring to Indian communities in the United States. Of the approximately 561 tribes in the United States alone, many refer to themselves in completely different ways. The nineteen Pueblo communities in New Mexico, for example, have distinct names such as San Juan Pueblo and Zia Pueblo. California is home to more than forty *rancherias*, or Indian communities located on small parcels of land, such as the Berry Creek Rancheria in Oroville and the Dry Creek Rancheria Band of Pomo Indians in Geyserville. *Rancherias*, like reservations in other states, are government-designated lands over which one or more

tribes maintain sovereignty. Farther north, many Native people of Alaska call their communities "villages." Examples are the Traditional Village of Togiak and Skagway Village.

There are many ways to refer to Native communities throughout the United States but even more ways to address the groups living to the north and south. Today Native people throughout Canada refer to themselves as aboriginal or members of First Nations rather than as American Indians or Native Americans. Each First Nation community in Canada has a specific name, such as the Swan Lake First Nation in Manitoba or the Peepeekisis Indian Band of Saskatchewan. In Mexico, Central America, and South America, indigenous cultures do not like to use the Spanish or Portuguese words for *Indian* or *tribe*, since the direct translations carry negative meanings. As a result, most Native people in these areas use the words *indígenas* ("indigenous people" or "indigenous") and *communidad* ("community") to describe who they are or where they come from.

It is important to remember that each Native tribe or nation has its own distinct viewpoint and culture. When identifying a Native community, first try to learn how members of the community describe themselves.

—TANYA THRASHER

WHY DO MANY TRIBES HAVE MORE THAN ONE NAME?

When Europeans arrived in the Americas, they discovered that Indians had named their particular nations in their own languages, which also specified names for rivers, mountains, trees, animals, plants, towns, and villages. Europeans found these names difficult to understand and pronounce. In time, original Indian personal names and place-names often were replaced by names chosen by the Spanish, German, Dutch, French, and English newcomers.

Thus, the names by which many Indian tribes are commonly known today likewise were not chosen by the tribes themselves. During the twentieth century some tribes cast off the names given to them by the French, Spanish, and English. For example, the Muscogee Nation, originally a confederacy of small tribes who lived in present-day Georgia and Alabama, were identified for several hundred years as the Creek Indians. This name was applied to them by English colonists because abundant waterways flowed through their lands.

Other communities rejected the often insulting nicknames that had originated with other tribes. In 1984 the tribe in southern Arizona formerly called Papago, a Spanish mispronunciation of a Native word meaning "bean-eaters," reverted to its traditional name: "Tohono O'odham," or "desert people." Many Dakota, Lakota, and Nakota peoples prefer these traditional names to "Sioux," or "little snakes," which is a French approximation of the name they were called by the Ojibwe, their tribal enemy. In 1992, the Navajo Nation's president, Peterson Zah, sponsored a resolution to change the official name of his tribe from "Navajo," which derives from a Tewa word that has been interpreted to mean either "people with large cornfields" or "people who steal."

"Diné," the new name, means simply "the people." That name, as well as "Diné Nation," signifies cultural pride.

Sometimes tribal names can become complex for outsiders. Many people mistakenly refer to the Iroquois as a tribe, but they are actually a confederacy of six tribes known as the Haudenosaunee. The nations that comprise the Haudenosaunee are the Mohawk, Onondaga, Cayuga, Seneca, Oneida, and Tuscarora. The Ojibwe people of the Great Lakes region are divided into bands and communities that prefer to be known as either Ojibwe, Chippewa, or—especially in Canada—Anishinaabe. Each of these names can be spelled in different ways. When referring to American Indian tribes, it is best to remain aware that names change and that all names carry meanings and histories that aren't always easily discernible.

—NEMA MAGOVERN AND EDWIN SCHUPMAN

How do I prove my Indian ancestry and enroll in my tribe?

In 2006 each of the 561 federally recognized tribes in the United States had a sovereign government with its own way of identifying tribal members and permitting individuals to become new members. Most tribes today require that members have one-quarter or one-half "blood quantum," which means that at least one grandparent or parent is a member of the particular tribe. Other tribes require very little blood quantum. Still others grant membership based on family lineage—memberships may be passed down only from a mother or only from a father. The Cherokee Nation of Oklahoma determines individual membership by whether a person's ancestor's name was on the Dawes Roll, a census taken at the turn of the twentieth century that listed Cherokee people who were eligible for land allotments. The most important idea, however, is that each tribe establishes its membership in a different way. Tribes have the right—because they are governments—to decide who is and who is not a tribal member. As a result, a lot of Native people today may not "look Indian" or fit the stereotypical image of an Indian.

Before the federal government became involved, membership was determined solely by tribes and not necessarily by the amount of Native "blood" (blood quantum) an individual possessed. Even today, tribes can adopt people who don't have the required blood quantum. But determination of tribal membership by blood quantum has endured since the 1800s mainly because the federal government, in establishing the reservation system, insisted that commodity foodstuffs be issued only to those who could prove they were Native American. As a result, American Indian peoples are the only group in the United States today who require proof (via tribal enrollment cards) of identity.

In Canada, before laws were amended in 1985, the federal government officially decided who was and was not an Indian by controlling the membership lists of tribal bands. After 1985 about 250 out of Canada's approximately six hundred bands, which are also called First Nations, opted to control their own memberships. The federal government still retains the right to identify individual "Status" and "non-Status" Indians, which in turn determines the government benefits for which an individual may be eligible. To be granted Indian status, a person usually has to be a member of a band that has already negotiated a treaty with the government or been granted a reserve or government funds.

In Mesoamerica and South America, intermarriage between indigenous and European peoples began soon after Columbus's arrival in 1492. Successive generations became known as mestizos, who now make up a large part of the populations of Mexico, Guatemala, Ecuador, Peru, Bolivia, and other countries. In these nations, being indigenous has become more a cultural and political than a biological distinction, with the term *indígenas* identifying those who have not abandoned their traditional dress and cultural practices. Official systems of tribal enrollment have never been established, either by the federal governments or by indigenous peoples, but in some South American countries indigenous communities have banded together into strong political federations. The communities themselves almost always know who their people are.

People in the United States who believe they are descended from a particular tribe have many references to consult. American Indians—by virtue of their special historical relationship with the federal government—are among the world's most well-documented peoples. One should start by pinpointing the tribe from which one believes he or she is descended. A variety of official records, such as birth, marriage, and other family documents, can be researched. Schools and churches are also resources for information about ancestors. Government records at the National Archives and Records Administration can be consulted once an ancestor's tribe has been specified. Tribes, which have offices that deal with these types of inquiries, can also help, once it has been determined that the ancestor in question was a member of that tribe.

—LIZ HILL

ARE THERE SPECIAL TRADITIONS SURROUNDING NATIVE AMERICAN BABY-NAMING?

At a time when picking baby names has become a popular ritual, American Indian naming traditions stand out for their originality and tribal specificity. Truly, Native Americans show that one does not have to be born yesterday to receive a name. In fact, in some North Pacific Coast communities, members are aged forty-five to sixty by the time they receive their official names. Traditionally, the Delaware also delayed naming, waiting until a child was three or four years old to ensure that the Creator intended the child to live.

In many Native American traditions, naming comes long after birth and often. Before the reservation system was established, an individual's name changed many times throughout life to mark important events and accomplishments. For centuries, Hopi individuals have received new names at birth, childhood, adulthood, and death. In the Hopi baby-naming ceremony, two ears of corn representing "Mother Corn" are placed beside the newborn for nineteen days. On the twentieth day, the baby's grandmother puts a pinch of cornmeal into the baby's mouth and gives the baby a name. Later in life, Hopi individuals receive new names when they are initiated into *katsina* organizations. It is important to acknowledge that the Hopi people are not alone in maintaining their practice of naming. Tribes throughout the hemisphere continue to follow the specific naming customs of their cultures.

What is a naming ceremony like? It depends on the tribe. In Ojibwe culture, parents seek an elder or spiritual leader who fasts, dreams, or meditates to receive the name from the Spirit World. In a gathering of family and friends, that person then offers tobacco to the four directions and reveals the name. While every tribe has its

own customs, some common practices during a naming ceremony are feasting, cleansing, smudging, socializing, and dancing. Giveaways are also often part of a naming ceremony, as a way for the family holding the event to thank the guests for carrying the name into the future. In Haudenosaunee (Iroquois) culture, names revert to the person's clan after death.

Overall, the practices of Native American naming contrast with those that most people around the world experience. If you were to be named in a Native American tradition, it might not be your parents who name you; you might be named long after birth and acquire new names as you grow older; you might have names that are reserved for special occasions; or you might have a name that is never meant to be spoken at all. There are many possibilities but no comprehensive "rule book." As a result, contemporary Native Americans have names that are indigenous, English, or any combination, and a story can be told for every individual.

—JENNIFER ERDRICH

Why is the word SQUAW offensive?

Indians of all tribes in the United States and Canada reject the use of *squaw* as the word for an Indian woman. Beginning in the early 1620s, English colonists borrowed the word *squa* from Massachusett, an Algonquian language spoken by the indigenous peoples of eastern Massachusetts. In that language, *squa* meant simply "female" or "younger woman." In the neighboring Mohawk language, however, the word *ojiskwa'* can be translated as "vagina." In 1973, scholars Thomas E. Sanders and Walter W. Peek argued that *squaw* had evolved from that meaning rather than from the Massachusett.

Over the past four hundred years the word has been used in a derogatory manner and has taken on negative meanings. During the nineteenth century, American writers tended to classify Indian women as "princesses" or "squaws," the latter described in James Fenimore Cooper's *Last of the Mohicans* as "the crafty 'squaw' . . . the squalid and withered person of this hag." Today it is not easy to find an Indian woman who accepts being called a squaw.

More than a thousand locales in the United States have the word *squaw* in their names. One of the best known was Squaw Peak, on the outskirts of Phoenix, Arizona. For six years State Senator Jack Jackson, a Navajo member of the Arizona legislature, repeatedly introduced a bill to rename the mountain but was met each time with strong resistance. In 1998, after several months of public discussion, the Arizona Board on Geographic and Historic Names voted down a proposal to change the name to Iron Mountain but left open the possibility of a future name change. In 2003, when Army Pfc. Lori Piestewa (Hopi) of Tuba City, Arizona, became the

first Native servicewoman ever killed in combat, "Squaw Peak" was renamed, with nearly no dissent, to Piestewa Peak.

Although similar name changes—such as the transformation of Squaw Lake in Minnesota to Nokomis Lake Pond—have not come as easily, Native protest against the word has intensified. While some American Indians say that they can accept *squaw* in certain contexts, most feel the word is as offensive as any racist term and should be consigned to linguistic history.

—GEORGETTA STONEFISH RYAN

Why is the word *Eskimo* sometimes offensive?

There are eleven different cultural groups in Alaska, so the word *Eskimo* is used there to refer to all Inuit and Yup'ik peoples, who live throughout the world's northernmost regions. But the name is considered insulting in many places outside Alaska because it was given by non-Inuit people and said to mean "eater of raw meat." Linguists now believe that *Eskimo* is derived from an Ojibwe word meaning "to net snowshoes." The Inuit people of Canada and Greenland, however, prefer other names. *Inuit,* meaning "people," is used in most of Canada, and the Inuit people of Greenland call themselves *Greenlanders,* or *Kalaallit* in their language.

Most Alaskans continue to accept the name *Eskimo* because, within the state, *Inuit* refers only to the Inupiat of northern Alaska. If a person's specific Alaskan cultural group isn't known, however, it's best for outsiders to use the term *Alaska Native.*

—MARY AHENAKEW

WHAT'S WRONG WITH NAMING SPORTS TEAMS INDIANS, BRAVES, ETC.?

Gooooooo *Indians! Yea, Redskins!* These are just two of the chants one may hear at sports events, when one or both of the teams are identified by Native American names or related terminology, which is often the case. One might also see fans practicing "tomahawk chops" or wearing "war paint" and feathers. You might even see a Muppet-like character dressed in "Indian" garb as the team mascot, whooping, hollering, and jumping around. This "in-your-face" mockery of Indian identity can easily lead to racist incidents.

Since the arrival of Europeans, Native Americans have struggled for survival. Indian people are often still seen as part of the past and unrelated to the present or future. The approximately 4 million Native Americans in the United States are not a big consideration for politicians seeking votes or corporations marketing to the public. Terms such as *redskins, warriors, scalping, braves, squaw,* and *chiefs* belittle hundreds of diverse Indian cultures, reducing them to a single stereotype that can be easily exploited by anyone in search of an identifiable brand. Currently, no other ethnic group in the United States suffers from this sort of openly racist treatment.

Many professional and amateur sports teams still use Native American names, even though Native American people have strongly objected. Thousands of people, many of them non-Indians, and more than eighty organizations—including the National Congress of American Indians, the Rainbow Coalition, the American Psychological Association, and the National Education Association—have advocated for change. And change has occurred: since 1970, when the University of Oklahoma became the first school to eliminate its "Little Red"

Indian mascot, more than two-thirds of the three thousand schools with Indian sports names and mascots have followed suit.

Perhaps the most objectionable of all sports-team names is that of the Washington, D.C., pro-football team, the Redskins. Partly because of the team's location in the nation's capital, and partly because the term is considered a racial slur, the Washington Redskins's name has been a particular target of complaint. The most sustained of these protests is a fourteen-year lawsuit brought by Suzan Shown Harjo (Cheyenne/Hodulgee Muscogee), president of the Morningstar Institute, a Native rights foundation, and six prominent Native co-plaintiffs. A panel of three judges canceled the football team's trademark licenses in 1999, but the decision was overturned in 2003 by a judge who ruled that the plaintiffs should have filed their suit when the team's trademarks were first registered, in 1967. After noting that Mateo Romero, the youngest of the plaintiffs, was only one year old in 1967, the D.C. Circuit Court of Appeals ruled in 2005 that the case had been prematurely dismissed. Harjo and her co-plaintiffs were given another chance to demonstrate that the Redskins trademarks do, in fact, disparage American Indians.

The issue of Indian sports mascots is not always as clear-cut. In August 2005 the National Collegiate Athletic Association (NCAA) ruled that member schools could not use "hostile and abusive" Native mascots at any of the eighty-eight NCAA championship events. The eighteen colleges and universities affected by the decision would either have to change their mascots or use them only during the regular season. Since then, at least four schools, including the Florida State Seminoles and the University of Southern Utah Utes, have won appeals because at least one band of their "namesake" tribe supports the schools' current use of names and logos.

Nevertheless, in a poll conducted in 2001 by the newspaper *Indian Country Today*, 81 percent of respondents felt that the use of American Indian names, symbols, and mascots is deeply offensive to American Indians. When a people's identity is reduced to caricatures or mascots, their real concerns can be more easily dismissed.

—STEPHANIE BETANCOURT

WHAT IS THE ORIGIN OF THE TERM *REDSKIN*? WHY IS IT OFFENSIVE?

Many scholars attribute the term *redskin* to naturalists in mid-1700s Europe who were busy creating classifications for everything and everybody. Carolus Linnaeus, a Swedish naturalist, decided to use primary colors to label the four races of mankind: *Europaeus albus* (white), *Americanus rubescens* (red), *Asiaticus fuscus* (yellow), and *Africanus niger* (black). His labels, described in successive editions of his work *Systema Naturae* (1735), were widely accepted. Another scholar, Alden T. Vaughn, contends that the color red was associated with the red body paint that many Indians wore, and he concludes, "In the middle of the nineteenth century, anthropologist Henry Rowe Schoolcraft's *Oneóta, or, Characteristics of the Red Race of America* (1845) and James Fenimore Cooper's *The Redskins* (1846) symbolically marked Caucasian America's full recognition, in both fiction and science, of Indians as innately red and racially distinct."

An Indian view of the origins of the term *redskin* is expressed by writer Suzan Shown Harjo, who offers a visual scenario: Just imagine that it is 1756 and you are being tracked by bounty hunters. But you have committed no crime. A bounty has been placed on you simply because you are an Indian and live on coveted land. The bounty hunter finds you, murders you, and scalps you. Then he turns in your bloody scalp (that's where the red in the term *redskin* comes from) and collects his pay. Decapitated heads were also accepted.

Redskin is offensive to most Indian people, yet it continues to be used today. The name of the Washington Redskins football team is one example.

—MARY AHENAKEW

Is it true that Indians do not like to have their photographs taken because they believe the camera might steal their spirit?

For American Indians, belief in the camera's ability to capture an individual's spirit may be more a personal conviction than a tribal one. Spirit capture can be linked to the idea, prevalent in some tribes, of the spirit as a distinct entity that can become detached from the body. But mistaking an individual's reluctance to be photographed for fear of "spirit capture" reduces intricate ideas about cosmology and personhood to superstition.

Photography came of age in a time of great upheaval for Native Americans. By the late 1800s Native people in the East had endured colonization for hundreds of years, and many already had been forced to move from their eastern homelands across the Mississippi River. Tribes in the West were battling the government to maintain their lifeways and protect traditional lands from encroaching settlers, including the displaced eastern tribes. As the federal government was forcing these western tribes onto reservations, photography—which had arrived in North America in 1839—was becoming more accessible and portable. As journalists, anthropologists, documentarians, artists, and tourists invaded Indian Country in pursuit of the newly tamed "wild Indian" or to document the last vestiges of a "vanishing race," Native people became increasingly wary of the ways in which photographers were transforming their lives into spectacle.

In the late 1800s and early 1900s, railroad companies and tour operators set out to entice tourists to the newly "opened" Southwest. One of the features they promoted was a staged version of Indian life that emphasized peaceful artisanship and supposedly exotic rituals. The Hopi Snake and Antelope ceremony, more commonly known as the Hopi Snake Dance, was a particularly popular attraction because

Princess Theresia of Bavaria, photographing
Indian performers at the Buffalo Bill Wild
West show, 1890. Munich, Bavaria.

Photo by Frank Lehner. P10218.

non-Indians perceived it as a connection to a wild, primitive paganism.
But many people who photographed the Snake Dance abused their
privilege. A photographer named George Wharton James, for example,
insisted on taking pictures inside sacred underground structures called
kivas, even after being specifically asked not to do so. He then sold the
images of this highly religious ceremony for personal gain. His action
led to a total ban on public viewing of the ceremony.

Photography continues to produce mixed emotions among American Indians. The camera's ability to preserve and document has also
been used to appropriate images and traditions. Anthropologists and
photojournalists remove sacred, privileged knowledge from its context and make it public. Shutterbug tourists show disrespect when
photographing without asking permission. Photodocumentarians, of
whom Edward Curtis is the most famous, limited by their personal
interpretations, often have perpetuated stereotypes.

Native people, however, have been reappropriating their images
for decades. Many tribes have closed off their ceremonies to outsiders
or placed strict guidelines on photographing events. At powwows the

protocol for taking photos of individual dancers requires that permission first be granted by the individual.

In addition to assuming more control of the photos non-Natives take of them, Native people are increasingly becoming professional photographers themselves. Horace Poolaw (Kiowa) was one of the earliest Native photographers, beginning his occupation in the early 1920s. He documented the lives of Native people as they made the transition from their traditional lifeways into the twentieth century. Another documentarian, Lee Marmon (Laguna Pueblo), began photographing Laguna tribal elders in the 1940s. Some Native photographers make cultural and political statements. Jolene Rickard (Tuscarora) uses photographic and digital media to explore her traditional Haudenosaunee (Iroquois) culture, comment on non-Native perceptions of Native life, and illustrate Native peoples' connection to the land. Rather than scrutinize their Native subjects as "others," Native artists create a dialogue between themselves, their subjects, and their audience. Whether as artists or people taking everyday snapshots, Native photographers document the lives and traditions of Native people, convey the power of the sacred landscape, and create social commentary with their cameras. They have a vested interest in preserving the sanctity of ceremonies— by not photographing them—while they "capture" with their cameras the beauty and multidimensionality of Native daily life.

—ARWEN NUTTALL

ORIGINS
AND
HISTORIES

WHERE DID INDIANS COME FROM? HOW DID THEY GET TO THE AMERICAS?

For thousands of generations, Native communities throughout the Americas have affirmed the creation of each nation on its land. According to a creation story told in the Northeast, the world began when Sky Woman fell from her home in the heavens. Birds flew under her to prevent her fall, and they placed her on the back of a great turtle, giving her a safe landing. Mud brought by the muskrat became the entire world, providing Sky Woman's descendants with a place to live—the eastern woodlands. In the Northwest, Raven coaxed little people to come out of their hiding places in the earth, while in southeastern North America, Crow pecked at shells and, in opening them, released people upon the earth. The stories vary in their details, but all convey the idea that Native people have always lived in the Americas. Oral histories give meaning to beliefs in a way that can be memorized and retold, and they emphasize the presence of a creative force that permeates humans, animals, and the land.

In contrast, the long-held scientific theory focuses on migration. Popularly called the Bering Strait theory, it asserts that ancestors of American Indians gradually came to North America from Asia between about twelve thousand and sixty thousand years ago. According to this school of thought, nomadic peoples journeyed from Asia to North America at various times during the last ice age, when sea levels were lower and the land underneath what is known today as the Bering Strait (a narrow body of water between Siberia and Alaska, near the Arctic Circle) was exposed. This thousand-mile-wide "land bridge" probably supported migrations in both directions. Similarities in the spear points used in Asia and those found in the southwestern area of North America, and similarities in the physical traits of Asians and

American Indians, have been the primary pieces of evidence that support this theory. More recently, geneticists have been tracing DNA markers, which tend to indicate various waves of migration. Over many generations, it is postulated, nomadic hunters followed game animals such as mammoths, elks, moose, and caribou across the land bridge, eventually (once the longer-lasting inland glaciers had receded) fanning out to settle the entire Western Hemisphere.

In 1996 the oldest known skeleton in North America—Kennewick Man—was discovered near the Columbia River in Washington State. The region's Native people claim the ninety-two-hundred-year-old remains as an honored ancestor and wish to rebury them. This has brought the remains to the center of a dispute between the tribes and some anthropologists, who want to study the bones for their potential to shed light on early immigrants to North America. Some scientists have suggested that the skull of the Kennewick Man most closely resembles those of Polynesian and Ainu peoples of Asia. If confirmed, this proposal might support the theory that a migration route followed the shoreline of the North Pacific at a time when inland routes were still icebound. This in turn implies that at least some of the continent's earliest settlers may have arrived by boat rather than on foot via the Bering land bridge.

Open to further study is the possibility that North America was populated by migration from Mesoamerica and South America. Corn cultivation, textile skills, rubber ball games, and other sociocultural developments in the Western Hemisphere began in Mesoamerica and the Andes. For instance, it is known that squashes were being cultivated by about 8700 BC in Mexico and by 2500 BC in eastern North America. Although the crop may have been developed separately by two indigenous groups, the seeming migration of squashes and other cultivated plants suggests the gradual northward migration of humans. Still, the question remains: Where did South Americans themselves originate? Recent archaeological discoveries in the Andes suggest humans may have inhabited South America far earlier than previously thought, more than thirty thousand years ago.

Many American Indians reject the various migration theories, wary that they could be used to portray Native people as immigrant settlers who happened to arrive earlier than their European "counterparts." By dismissing as unscientific the creation stories that spiritually bind Native communities to the land, non-Native scholars and educators reinforce the idea that Europeans were simply another wave of immigrants who had the right to displace the Americas' previous inhabitants. In 1995 the late Vine Deloria Jr. (Standing Rock

Sioux) wrote, "By making us immigrants to North America, [non-Indians] are able to deny the fact that we were the full, complete, and total owners of this continent. They are able to see us simply as earlier interlopers and therefore throw back at us the accusation that we had simply *found* North America a little earlier than they had."

The scientific quest for knowledge about the origins of the earliest inhabitants of the Western Hemisphere is far from conclusive. Some researchers in the new science of geomythology are turning to Native traditional tales as a source of knowledge about climatic and geologic events of the distant past. As scientific theories continue to be refined, however, Native people will likely also continue to provide the same answer to this question as have generations of their ancestors: "We have always been here, from time immemorial."

—RICO NEWMAN AND GEORGETTA STONEFISH RYAN

How Many Indians Lived in the Western Hemisphere When Columbus Arrived?

Nobody knows the exact population of the Western Hemisphere at the time Europeans first arrived, but the question has been keenly debated by historians for nearly a century. The first scholarly estimate of an indigenous population was made in 1910 by James Mooney, a Smithsonian ethnographer who, relying on historical documents, concluded that the population of America north of Mexico in 1491 was about 1.15 million people. This number now appears exceedingly low.

In 1966, Henry F. Dobyns published an article in the journal *Current Anthropology* that pieced together the devastating effect on Native people of the diseases unleashed by the arrival of Europeans in North and South America. Beginning in 1525, smallpox wiped out more than half the population of the Inka empire. During the following century, typhus, diphtheria, and measles added to the toll. The diseases spread inland, even to communities that had never been visited by white people. Dobyns estimated that in the first 130 years after Contact, Native America lost about 95 percent of its population. When the French, the English, and the Spanish arrived in parts of the Americas, they were mystified by empty villages. In other regions the land seemed untouched by human inhabitants.

From his evidence, Dobyns concluded that the Indian population of North America in 1491 was about 18 million and the hemisphere's populations about 90 million, but the figures continue to be disputed. More recently, Russell Thornton, in his book *American Indian Holocaust and Survival* (1987), surveys the estimates of other anthropologists and demographers and offers an estimate of approximately 75 million for the Western Hemisphere in 1492. No one can be certain

of the death toll exacted by the initial waves of disease, but succeeding epidemics, warfare, forced relocations, and harsh living conditions continued to reduce Indian populations over the next four hundred years. Many historians believe that the Native population of the United States reached its lowest point—about 250,000—at the end of the nineteenth century. In the last hundred years, it has rebounded to about 4.1 million.

European explorers and settlers who first arrived in the "New World" wanted to believe it was just that: new not only to them but to all humankind. With their diseases preceding them, diminishing complex Native civilizations, Europeans readily assumed that the Americas were, and always had been, a barely populated wilderness. This view, which justified hundreds of years of European land theft and mistreatment of Indians, has been slow to die. As late as 1987, a standard high school textbook described American history as "the story of the creation of a civilization where none existed."

—STEPHANIE BETANCOURT

WHAT WERE SOME OF THE ACCOMPLISHMENTS OF NATIVE AMERICANS AT THE TIME EUROPEANS FIRST ARRIVED IN THE WESTERN HEMISPHERE?

The first European explorers in the Western Hemisphere, including Christopher Columbus, remarked on the ingenuity of the indigenous population, claiming at times that its accomplishments surpassed those found in the Old World. But unable to find weapons, metal tools, or Christianity on the continent they had "discovered," Europeans for the most part characterized Native people as ignorant and heathenish.

Most history textbooks begin at 1492, ignoring the significant accomplishments of pre-Contact Native Americans. With specialized tradesmen and artisans as well as populous cities and economic stratification, European society may have seemed more advanced than the villages and even the cities of the Western Hemisphere. But filth and disease pervaded Renaissance Europe. Wars for land, wealth, and power destabilized European political and daily life, and religious intolerance led to injustice and brutality.

Native societies may have lacked metal tools and weapons, domesticated animals, or large-scale agriculture in the 1500s, but they were highly resourceful and adaptable to the varied environments of the Western Hemisphere. As for agriculture, many of the staple foods grown today, including corn, potatoes, tomatoes, squashes, peanuts, and chilies, were first cultivated by Native people and carried to Europe, Africa, and Asia by Europeans. Although Europeans created the process for making the sweet chocolate we eat today, the Maya and the Aztec were grinding cacao beans to create a sugarless beverage long before the arrival of Columbus. It was some of these nutritious food exports from the Americas that provided a boost to Europe's population, which had never fully

recuperated from the human devastation of the Black Death in the 1300s.

The domestication of animals in Southwest Asia ten thousand years ago introduced many diseases to the human population. In the crowded, unhygienic urban centers of Europe, diseases spread quickly. In contrast, the Western Hemisphere had few infectious diseases. Communities in the American Southwest made soap and shampoo out of yucca. The Shoshone sterilized their surgical spaces hundreds of years before Western doctors recognized the spread of germs as a source of infection during surgery. More than fifty present-day prescription drugs have been developed by studying the ways in which plant extracts were used in traditional Native medicine. Most of the plants from which these medicines are derived are native to the Amazonian rain forest, an area where contemporary indigenous peoples are facing the encroachment of pharmaceutical companies, pressures from local and foreign governments, and sometimes murder by loggers and miners.

Pre-Contact Native societies were also responsible for extensive road networks, such as those found in the Andes and southwestern North America as well as for architectural feats such as the Mississippian mounds and the Mesoamerican pyramids. The Olmec people of Mesoamerica invented rubber, an entrancing innovation to the conquistadores. One of the most important systems of government in the world today was developed by the Haudenosaunee (Iroquois). The Great Law of Peace, which may have appeared as early as AD 1142, described a democratic system in which the leader's political power is balanced by the rights of the individual.

While the moment of first contact between the Eastern and Western Hemispheres is usually told as the story of Columbus's "discovery" of the Americas, its far-reaching effects have made it probably the single most important event in history. In myriad ways, it changed the fabric of global life.

—ARWEN NUTTALL

WHO REALLY BUILT THE MOUNDS?

Mounds, or man-made earthworks, hundreds of feet in length and height can be found throughout what is now the eastern, midwestern, and southern United States, from Minnesota to Florida and New England to Louisiana. Upon first encountering the mounds in the 1700s and 1800s, Europeans variously attributed the feat of building them to early Spanish explorers; an ancient, vanished civilization; the lost tribes of Israel; Vikings; and the survivors of the lost city of Atlantis. Noting similarities to stone edifices in Mesoamerica, late nineteenth-century scientists speculated that the Maya and the Aztec civilizations had extended farther north than previously supposed. Seeing no contemporaneous signs of a populous, specialized society that could have supported such an endeavor, explorers and archaeologists discounted any notion that American Indians had constructed the mounds.

In the twentieth century it became clear to archaeologists that the ancestors of the region's indigenous peoples had indeed constructed the mounds without help from abroad. Between about AD 700 and 1700 the Natchez people of the lower Mississippi Valley built enormous and numerous flat-topped mounds, constructing houses and temples on the broad plateaus. The nation's leader, called the Great Sun, lived on the largest mound, orchestrating the orderly conduct of daily life. The mounds were also used as burial chambers. Elaborate ceremonies and cultural disciplines were formulated and followed, both in building the mounds and burying the dead.

The logistics required to accomplish these feats of construction are staggering. Monk's Mound, for example, covering sixteen acres in southwestern Illinois, is the largest pre-Columbian earthwork in North

Aerial view of the Great Serpent Mound, ca.
1935. Adams County, Ohio.

Photo by Major Dache M. Reeves. P13211.

America. Larger at its base than the Great Pyramid at Giza, the mound still astonishes archaeologists with its sheer size.

In the nineteenth century, with most indigenous nations forced to move west of the Mississippi, Europeans, intent on possessing the fertile lands, used or moved the mound soil to make way for farming. In the process, they destroyed many mounds. Some farmed on the broad surface of mounds, their plows uprooting human remains and burial goods. With such discoveries, looting proliferated, and many of the burial objects (including human bones) found their way into private and institutional collections.

The most renowned mound sites today are Cahokia, including Monk's Mound in Illinois, and Serpent Mound in the Ohio Valley. State and federal officials have passed laws to prevent looting, and in several states mounds are tourist attractions that draw thousands of visitors each year. Continued preservation of the mounds is an open question, owing to the cost of maintaining them. In addition, wind, snow, and rain have had a constant effect, causing erosion over time.

Indigenous nations with different languages, social conventions, and forms of leadership had a remarkably similar need to construct these monuments. Their systems and techniques remain the subjects of speculation. Questions about population, group discipline, work assignment, time of construction, methods for moving soil, workforce, and the ability to sustain interest and health over time remain unanswered. In the end, the mounds are an enduring testament to the skills, knowledge, social developments, religious and spiritual beliefs, discipline, and order of Native societies before Europeans arrived in North America.

—RICO NEWMAN

WHAT IS THE SIGNIFICANCE OF THE SWASTIKA FOR NATIVE AMERICANS?

Today it is natural to associate this symbol with the brutality of the Nazis and the horrors of the Holocaust, but in ancient times—and still in Buddhist and Hindu cultures—the swastika represented life, sun, power, strength, and good luck. Of the many forms of the cross found throughout the world, the swastika is one of the most ancient. Despite a long history of scholarly theory and speculation, its origin is unknown. The symbol, which has been in use for more than three thousand years in Asia and Europe, was first discovered in North America on stone, shell, and metal ornaments found at archaeological sites in Tennessee, Georgia, and Ohio. The name *swastika* comes from the Sanskrit word, *svastika*, with *sv* meaning "good" or "well," and *asti* meaning "to be," "being," or "it is."

The swastika, or its reversed version, called a *sauvastika*, can be found in Navajo weavings and Pueblo pottery. It decorates the ceremonial objects and garments of the Kickapoo, Sac, Potawatomi, and Iowa people, for whom it is a symbol of good luck. For the Coast Salish people of British Columbia, it is a sign of the four winds.

The sauvastika has sometimes been associated with misfortune and bad luck, but it can also represent friendship. For the Mohawks, the sauvastika symbolizes the North Star.

—MARY AHENAKEW

The swastika, or a reversed version called a sauvastika, symbolized in ancient times life, sun, power, strength, and good luck, but since World War II, the design has disappeared from most Native art. For Coast Salish people, the swastika represents the four winds.

Skokomish basket with four winds motif, ca. 1900. Tulalip Reservation, Washington. Red cedar root, wild cherry bark, and nettle root.

Photo by Ernest Amoroso. 5/7926.

WHAT IS THE SIGNIFICANCE OF THE SWASTIKA FOR NATIVE AMERICANS?

35

IS IT TRUE THAT INDIANS SOLD MANHATTAN FOR TWENTY-FOUR DOLLARS WORTH OF BEADS AND TRINKETS?

The "sale" of Manhattan was a misunderstanding. In 1626 the director of the Dutch settlement, Peter Minuit, "purchased" Manhattan for sixty guilders worth of trade goods. At that time Indians did everything by trade, and they did not believe that land could be privately owned, any more than could water, air, or sunlight. But they did believe in giving gifts for favors done. The Lenni Lenape—one of the tribes that lived on the island now known as Manhattan—interpreted the trade goods as gifts given in appreciation for the right to share the land. We don't know exactly what the goods were or exactly how much a guilder was worth at that time. It has been commonly thought that sixty guilders equaled about twenty-four dollars. But the buying power of twenty-four dollars in 1626 is not known for sure.

To Europeans, ownership of land was synonymous with wealth, power, and prestige. To purchase land meant that the purchaser had the exclusive right to own and use it. The Lenni Lenape did not realize that the Dutch meant to hold the land for their exclusive use. In 1653, Dutch colonists put up a wall across lower Manhattan to protect the north side of their settlement from attacks by Indian tribes and the British. By 1700 the British had taken over the Dutch colony, torn down the barrier, and built in its place a paved lane called Wall Street.

At the time the Lenni Lenape (which translates as "the people") occupied lands now known as the states of Delaware, New Jersey, lower New York State, lower Connecticut, and the western tip of Long Island. Not long before the supposed sale of Manhattan, a man named Captain Samuel Argall found a large bay on the Atlantic Coast north of the Chesapeake Bay. He named it in honor of Sir

An artist's rendition of a scene in which
Peter Minuit (1580–1638), the director of the
Dutch colony of New Netherland, offers a
group of Native villagers a variety of goods
from a chest in exchange for Manhattan
Island, May 24, 1626.

Thomas West, the third Lord de la Warre, who was the governor of
the Virginia colony. The bay, the river, the governed territory, and the
local Indians all became known by the name Delaware.

—GEORGETTA STONEFISH RYAN

Is it true that Pocahontas saved John Smith from being executed?

Historians disagree, but the general consensus is that John Smith's story about his rescue is probably not true.

"Pocahontas" was actually a nickname, one of four names that the famous Indian girl had throughout her life. Although known today as Pocahontas, meaning "mischievous one," her given name was Amonute. Yet she also kept the secret spiritual name Matoaka, and when baptized and married she took the name Rebecca. She was never able to tell her own story, but Pocahontas's legend endures four hundred years later and grows stronger with each new generation. As an eleven- or twelve-year-old girl in the early 1600s, and one of the many children of the ruling chief Powhatan of present-day Virginia, Pocahontas lived during a time of great change for her people—a time of war and struggle with the English colonists of the Jamestown settlement.

Although little is known about her, aside from that provided by English sources, there is still much more to the story of young Pocahontas than today's films and storybooks tell. These dramatic (and largely false) versions usually describe Pocahontas as a mature woman in her twenties, who fell deeply in love with colonist John Smith and heroically saved his life. In truth, she was a much younger girl when she met Smith, and her connection to him was likely not a romantic one. Facts that remain important milestones in the young woman's life are her abduction by colonists and her life as a captive aboard an English ship; her eventual conversion to Christianity, her marriage to Englishman John Rolfe and the birth of a son named Thomas; and her celebrated visit to the court of King James I in England—all before her death at the tender age of twenty-two.

Unknown artist, probably after a 1616 engraving by Simon van de Passe (1595–1647).
Pocahontas (ca. 1595–1617).

National Portrait Gallery, Smithsonian Institution; gift of the A.W. Mellon Educational and Charitable Trust. NPG.65.61.

The details of Pocahontas's life are still actively debated among scholars and historians, the most frequently discussed question being whether Pocahontas threw herself across John Smith at his execution, pleading for mercy. Interestingly, the first person to recount the details of Pocahontas's life was Smith himself, when he began writing a "Generall Historie" of his experiences in America. Although he had published other accounts much earlier, the story of his "rescue" in AD 1607 from certain death by Pocahontas did not appear until 1624. Since its publication, Smith's vivid rescue story (by his account, Chief Powhatan would have smashed in his head with a stone ax if Pocahontas had not begged her father to spare him) has been vigorously challenged and doubted by many. But the story was adopted by other writers, who often romanticized it to appeal to eighteenth- and nineteenth-century readers.

No one knows for certain whether Smith's legendary rescue by Pocahontas actually occurred. Some scholars believe that Smith might have misunderstood what was happening to him, asserting that the elaborate ceremony taking place was actually a traditional adoption ceremony, bringing him into the tribe. But some historians maintain that the event could have taken place as Smith recalled it, and that he may well have been killed if Pocahontas had not intervened.

A more romanticized engraved portrait of Pocahontas, wearing a shawl, feathered headdress, and European-styled necklace.

Although the details of her rescue of (and relationship to) John Smith are not fully understood, it is widely accepted that Pocahontas was an important figure in American history who, despite her youth, contributed greatly to the early survival of the Jamestown colony.

—TANYA THRASHER

WHAT WAS THE IROQUOIS CONFEDERACY AND HOW DID IT CONTRIBUTE TO DEMOCRACY?

In the 1600s the Iroquois Confederacy was a political and military alliance comprising the original five nations of the Haudenosaunee, or "People of the Longhouse": the Seneca, Mohawk, Cayuga, Onondaga, and Oneida. In 1722 the Tuscarora, driven out of North Carolina, increased the number of participating nations to six. One of the largest—and most politically and militarily powerful—groupings of indigenous peoples in North America, the Haudenosaunee held territory that stretched some one thousand miles south to Kentucky and north to Quebec, east to Pennsylvania and west to Illinois. The document that laid out the Haudenosaunee Confederacy's system of government, or its constitution, was called the Great Law of Peace.

According to oral tradition, the Great Law of Peace, or Kaianere:kowa, was introduced to the Haudenosaunee people by Deganawidah, the "Peacemaker," who is said to have been a man of non-Iroquoian descent, and Ayonwatha (Hiawatha), a Mohawk or Onondaga, depending on the traditional version. The Great Law of Peace is an ancient document. In Haudenosaunee oral tradition, it appeared as early as AD 1142. According to Charles C. Mann, author of *1491: New Revelations of the Americas before Columbus* (2005), "The Haudenosaunee would have the second-oldest continuously existing representative parliament on earth. Only Iceland's Althing, founded in AD 930, is older." Further, as Emory Dean Keoke and Kay Marie Porterfield point out in an article about the Great Law in *American Indian* magazine (Fall 2004), "Many scholars believe the Great Law was the longest-lived international constitution at that time. The only possible exception to this was the unwritten English Constitution, which had its

origins in the English Magna Carta. Certainly, in fifteenth-century Europe nothing existed to rival this American Indian constitution."

The Haudenosaunee Confederacy was a consensus-driven form of government, meaning that all decisions that came before the confederacy had to be unanimous. The confederacy was represented by fifty sachems, or chiefs, chosen from among each of the Haudenosaunee nations. Its sessions were convened by the Todadaho, who represented the confederacy in diplomatic relations with other governments and who was always a member of the Onondaga Nation. Women, who headed the clans, chose the sachems (who were all men). The confederacy had the power to negotiate treaties but not to declare war.

The Great Law of Peace was by all accounts a sophisticated, effective, and modern system of governing, one in which political power was held in balance by an elaborate system of checks and a view of individual freedom that was truly revolutionary, at least for American settlers.

The constitution of the Haudenosaunee Confederacy made an indelible impression on the United States' Founding Fathers, including Benjamin Franklin, who used it as one model for the Articles of Confederation, which later were incorporated into the U.S. Constitution (ratified in 1789). In 1987 the U.S. Senate formally acknowledged, in a special resolution, the influence of the Haudenosaunee Great Law of Peace on the U.S. Constitution.

—LIZ HILL

DID EUROPEANS PURPOSELY USE SMALLPOX TO KILL INDIANS?

There is no clear evidence that the U.S. government ever used the smallpox virus to conduct a systematic, intentional extermination of Native peoples, but some tribal histories describe how some Europeans tried to wage war by accelerating the disease's spread. For example, the Crow Indian Tribe Resource Report issued on April 15, 2002, states that in 1843 "The United States used army blankets and rations festered with the small-pox germ and distributed [them] at Fort Parker." British soldiers, in one well-documented case at Fort Pitt, Pennsylvania, during the French and Indian wars, discussed the notion of spreading smallpox intentionally. With the approval of their commanders, soldiers gave to two chiefs some blankets and a handkerchief from a smallpox hospital. In 1763 Captain Simeon Ecuyler recorded the event in his journal, adding, "I hope it will have the desired effect."

Everywhere the Europeans landed, smallpox and other diseases quickly followed. Smallpox arrived as early as 1507 on the island of Hispaniola in the Caribbean, and the disease devastated the Taíno people of the Greater Antilles. In the mid-1520s two hundred thousand Andean Indians died. From 1616 to 1619 the disease hit coastal New England, decimating the population; in 1633 a smallpox epidemic struck the Narragansett peoples farther north along the eastern seaboard and quickly spread throughout the colonies. More than ten thousand Huron people of Ontario died. From 1780 to 1782 smallpox traveled through the Great Plains, affecting the Shoshone, Ojibwe, Blackfeet, Cree, Assiniboine, and many others. Around 1834 thousands of Chumash people in California died from the disease. In 1837–1838 smallpox almost entirely decimated the Mandan, Hidatsa, and Arikara

tribes along the Missouri River in present-day North Dakota. In 1840 the Crow were swept by the first of three smallpox epidemics that reduced the population from an estimated ten thousand to approximately two thousand in 1850. By 1853 the Makah people in Washington State had also been hit by the virus, as had a number of other Northwest Coast tribes.

In 1803 measures were already being taken to protect the U.S. military from smallpox and other infectious diseases in the Indian territories. Indians began to be provided with vaccinations against the smallpox virus in 1832, but the early vaccines may have caused more disease than they prevented.

As historian and Smithsonian curator Herman J. Viola notes in his book *After Columbus: The Smithsonian Chronicle of the North American Indians* (1990):

> Little wonder, then, that the Native Americans had no love for the European intruders. From North to South, East to West, the Indians shared the same tragedy, the same heartaches, the same feelings as the unknown Maya who lamented, "There was then no sickness; they had no aching bones; they had then no high fever; they had then no burning chest; they had then no abdominal pain; they had then no consumption; they had then no headache. At that time the course of humanity was orderly. The foreigners made it otherwise when they arrived here."

—LIZ HILL

WAS SACAGAWEA ALL THAT IMPORTANT TO THE LEWIS AND CLARK EXPEDITION?

Sacagawea, a young Shoshone woman who had been captured by the Mandan/Hidatsa people and was living among them, is often seen as a pivotal figure in the Lewis and Clark Expedition, which took place between 1804 and 1806. Sacagawea, who was about sixteen years old at the time, together with her husband—a French Canadian fur trader named Toussaint Charbonneau—and her infant son accompanied the American explorers Meriwether Lewis and William Clark on a journey ordered by President Thomas Jefferson that would take them from Fort Mandan on the Missouri River (land that became North Dakota) to the Pacific Ocean and back again. The primary purpose of the expedition was to find a western link in the (ultimately nonexistent) Northwest Passage, thought to be a waterway between the Atlantic and Pacific. Another purpose was to learn about the natural resources and Native tribes of the territory, so that trade could be established.

Over time Sacagawea's importance to the Lewis and Clark Expedition has taken on legendary proportions. It is true, however, that she was a valuable member of the party, identifying landmarks in her Shoshone homelands and helping to communicate with her people. Without Sacagawea, her brother Cameahwait would probably not have provided the expedition with goods and horses, taken them through Lemhi Pass, or saved them from a dangerous winter in the Rockies. In addition, her presence, and that of her baby, signaled to other tribes that Lewis and Clark's group was not a war party. She also had knowledge of a great variety of indigenous plants, which were useful sources of medicine and food.

The only written record of Sacagawea's life is in the journals

The head and tail sides of the U.S. dollar coin, 2000. The head side shows the likeness of Sacagawea and her infant son, Jean Baptiste. A bald eagle in flight surrounded by seventeen stars (the number of states in the Union at the time of Lewis and Clark's expedition) is featured on the tail side of the coin.

Lewis and Clark kept during their expedition, and very little is known about what happened to her after 1806. The date of Sacagawea's death is debated. Not only is her actual year of birth unknown—it is recorded as either 1786 or 1788—but also two death dates, years apart, are disputed. According to oral traditions, Sacagawea is said to have returned home to her Shoshone people, with whom she lived until her death in Wyoming in 1884. Another, more plausible, story reports her dying of a fever in 1812 at Fort Manuel in present-day South Dakota. Today Sacagawea remains among a handful of Native men and women who continue to fuel the popular imagination of many Americans for their courage and fortitude during one of the most important times in this country's history. To commemorate Sacagawea's bravery in a period when women were not recognized for their accomplishments, the first U.S. coin of the millennium featured her face and that of her baby.

—LIZ HILL

What Happened to White People Captured by Indians?

ince the 1700s stories have abounded of the terrible fates that befell innocent white maidens or courageous white frontiersmen and soldiers who were captured by American Indians supposedly hell-bent on rape, murder, and scalping. Catering to eighteenth- and nineteenth-century European stereotypes, the stories created romanticized legends of good (white settlers) versus evil (Indians). The stories—which appeared in newspapers, books, and popular journals, and later became staples of Wild West shows, movies, radio, and television—represented the righteous colonizers against the wild "other." What actually happened to white people captured by Native people varied from tribe to tribe, but the image of the murderous savage became a national myth that supported the theft of Native lands and the destruction of Native cultures.

Captivity stories are a documented part of North American history. Many are biased, however, overemphasizing or misinterpreting perceived negative aspects of Native society. Many books and the entertainment industry ignore the numerous accounts of white people who were captured by Indians, adopted into a tribe, and then wrenched unwillingly from their new families by their relatives or government soldiers. James Axtell, in his discussion of "white Indians," notes the case of John McCullough, a fourteen-year-old who had lived among the Shawnee in Ohio since the age of six. In 1764, while trying to forcibly remove McCullough from his community, the English "had his legs tied 'under the horses belly' and his arms tied behind his back with his father's garters, but to no avail." At first opportunity, McCullough escaped and returned to his Indian family, only to be recaptured a year later. When given the option to leave and return to the

Geronimo's band of Chiricahua Apaches abducted Santiago McKinn from his family's ranch in the Mimbres Valley, New Mexico, in 1885. Well treated, the boy assimilated to his new life, speaking Apache fluently and joining the other children in sports and games. When finally "rescued" in March 1886, he acted, according to Fletcher Lummis, a *Los Angeles Times* reporter, "like a young wild animal in a trap.... He bawled badly when told that he was to be taken back to his parents, and said he always wanted to stay with the Indians."

Cadmillus Sidney Fly. Santiago McKinn with Apache children, Canyon de los Embudos, Sonora, Mexico, March 1886.

Smithsonian Institution National Anthropological Archives.
SPC BAE 4605 01604807

white world, even many older adoptees preferred to stay with the tribe, shunning the entrapments of Anglo-European life.

White people came into the hands of Native people by several means, among them capture, adoption, marriage, and voluntary exchange. Some captives, usually the men, were killed for the violation of agreements, as retribution for the killing of tribal members, or to prevent the disclosure of settlement locations. Haudenosaunee (Iroquois) warriors sometimes forced their captives, en route to the victor's village, to run through a double row of villagers from allied tribes along the way, who hit and kicked the prisoners. Native tribes might eventually adopt their white captives, especially women and children. Adoption established ties of kinship and bestowed upon the captives membership in the community. A non-Native could then marry into a tribe and opt to follow the ways of his or her spouse's people. Stories also exist of lost children who were found and adopted by Native people.

Sometimes, white people were captured for the express purpose of prisoner exchange. Other times, Native headmen and government or military leaders would voluntarily exchange members to learn each other's language and customs. These volunteers could act as intermediaries during negotiations.

—ARWEN NUTTALL

WHY DIDN'T INDIAN TRIBES BAND TOGETHER TO FIGHT OFF EUROPEANS?

The rapid and devastating spread of European diseases is the main reason that Indian tribes were not able to unify against the European invaders. Another primary factor was the autonomy that most communities enjoyed. Hundreds of indigenous tribes were spread out across the continents. They spoke hundreds of different languages and governed their people in as many different ways. And, of course, not all the tribes were peaceful toward one another.

Imagine the Western Hemisphere—South, Central, and North America, including the Hawaiian Islands—as it might have been before the wave of European arrivals that began in the late 1400s. Some have estimated that the hemisphere's indigenous population numbered more than 70 million before this time. Great civilizations flourished, such as the Inka in South America, the Maya and Mexica (Aztec) in Central America and Mexico, and the Mississippian culture of North America. These societies—their immense populations and their activities were well documented by the Europeans who first came across them—were sophisticated and bustling centers of commerce, culture, and religion. But they were thousands of miles apart, separated by formidable geographic barriers.

An important point to keep in mind is that Europeans didn't arrive in the Americas all at once. In fact, even before Columbus landed in 1492, some of the Western Hemisphere's Native peoples had already seen light-skinned people. The Vikings, for example, visited the far northeastern part of the continent in AD 1000, a little less than five hundred years before Columbus. A number of tribes have centuries-old stories that mention white-skinned people.

Following Columbus's lead, Spanish explorers, including Hernando

The Shawnee leader Tecumseh
(ca. 1768–1813).

Hulton Archive, © 2004 Getty Images.

de Soto and Hernán Cortés, began more frequent travel between Europe and the Americas. With them came a variety of Old World diseases that spread with alarming rapidity to all corners of the Western Hemisphere in an extremely short time. Disease is now considered to be the major reason that Europeans—who came from much less populated countries (in 1492, Spain's population was only about 8 million) and who arrived with relatively few people aboard their ships—were able to overcome Native societies whose populations, particularly in South and Central America, were substantially larger.

Swept by epidemics of bubonic plague, smallpox, measles, cholera, and influenza, indigenous peoples, having no immunity, quickly fell ill and died in great numbers. In his book *Stolen Continents: The Americas through Indian Eyes since 1492* (1992), Ronald Wright writes, "The great death raged for more than a century. By 1600, after some twenty waves of pestilence had swept through the Americas, less than a tenth of the original population remained. Perhaps ninety million died, the equivalent, in today's terms, to the loss of a billion. It was the greatest mortality in history."

Disease is not the only reason that Europeans succeeded in taking over Native lands. Europeans brought with them metal weapons that had never been seen in the Americas, and they sometimes recruited tribes to fight with them against traditional enemies. The great Shawnee political and military leader, Tecumseh, championed the idea of Native political unity in 1810 and 1811, traveling from the Great Lakes to the Gulf of Mexico to promote concerted resistance to treaties that left Native nations with ever-diminishing lands. Few tribal chiefs, however, were interested in giving up their ability to negotiate directly with European and American governments.

—LIZ HILL

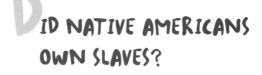ID NATIVE AMERICANS OWN SLAVES?

Individuals from some of the tribes that became known as the Five Civilized Tribes, including the Cherokee, Chickasaw, Choctaw, Creek, and Seminole, held African American slaves during the years leading up to the American Civil War. (The Seminole, however, later harbored runaway slaves, even accepting them into their communities.) These tribes—allies of the Confederacy during the Civil War—were labeled "civilized" by their non-Native neighbors because by the late 1700s and early 1800s they had adopted a number of non-Native customs. Characteristics of "civilization" included Christianity, European-style farming practices and homes, and written documents such as constitutions. The practice of enslaving Africans to provide labor on southern plantations was an accepted means of increasing wealth. Only gradually did slavery become a moral issue in the United States.

Slavery as an economic means to an end had been an alien concept to most Native people before contact with Europeans. Some experience of slavery, or servitude, however, had existed among indigenous populations, particularly among the wealth-conscious tribes of the North Pacific Coast. In the *Encyclopedia of North American Indians* (1996), Theda Perdue writes, "On the Northwest Coast, where material wealth assumed greater significance, slaves did acquire a value unknown elsewhere and became a species of property to be bought, sold, and given away."

In other parts of the country, once the economic benefits of selling slaves to the Europeans became known, a number of tribes began engaging in this practice, among them Native peoples of the Southwest, whose Indian slave trade intensified after the arrival of the

Spanish. The Catawba people in South Carolina also traded in slaves, as did a number of other southeastern tribes, which discovered early in the 1700s that the British were particularly eager to obtain slaves. Some of the more stratified societies of Caribbean, Central American, and South American peoples also included types of servitude. Slaves and servants often were former captives from neighboring Native tribes. Conditions varied a great deal, with slaves in some cultures gaining their liberty and even tribal honors.

—LIZ HILL

WHO WAS CHIEF SEATTLE? DIDN'T HE GIVE AN IMPORTANT SPEECH?

Sealth, Seat'tl, or Si' Al, as he was called (ca. 1786–1866), was a highly respected orator and leader of his people, the Duwamish of the Northwest Coast (in the area that is now Washington State). The city of Seattle is named after him.

Seattle, who was Suquamish on his father's side and Duwamish on his mother's side, lived during a time of great change for the Native peoples of the Northwest. Beginning with the arrival of British explorer George Vancouver's ship, HMS *Discovery*, at Puget Sound in 1792, the early 1800s brought great numbers of white settlers to the region. The settlers' encroachment on Native lands sparked conflicts between Indians and whites. Seattle was in the middle of it all.

By the early 1850s the first settlers, whom the Duwamish people called "Bostons," had migrated onto the land that would become known as the city of Seattle. In 1854, at the council with Governor Isaac Stevens for the Treaty of Point Elliot, Seattle delivered his famous farewell speech, which became part of the council minutes. Then he and his people left the area and went west across Puget Sound.

Seattle's speech was translated by physician and amateur writer Dr. Henry A. Smith, who was present and took notes. It would be more than thirty years, however, before Smith published his version in the *Seattle Sunday Star* newspaper—on October 29, 1887. Because the speech has been translated so many times over the years, scholars have debated how much of it was actually spoken by Seattle and how much embellished, even in the first translation by Smith. In 1972 a writer named Ted Perry wrote a fictional rendering of the speech for a television film about pollution. Perry's version, adopted by ecologists

Postcard of Chief Sealth
(Seattle [Duwamish], 1786–1866),
ca. 1900. Washington.

P16632

all over the world, has been another source of confusion. Despite the differences of opinion, it is agreed that the essence of Seattle's words has amounted to one of the most important orations ever delivered by an American Indian.

Here is one famous passage, excerpted from Smith's translation, that speaks to the reverence Seattle felt for the land and his people:

> Every part of this country is sacred to my people. Every
> hillside, every valley, every plain and grove has been hallowed
> by some fond memory or some sad experience of my tribe.
> Even the rocks, which seem to lie dumb as they swelter in the
> sun along the silent shore in solemn grandeur, thrill with
> memories of past events connected with the fate of my people.
> The very dust under your feet responds more lovingly to our
> footsteps than to yours, because it is the ashes of our ancestors
> and our bare feet are conscious of the sympathetic touch, for
> the soil is rich with the life of our kindred.

—LIZ HILL

For more information, visit the Suquamish Museum website at http://www.suquamish.nsn.us.

ARE INDIANS U.S. CITIZENS?

American Indians hold two distinct forms of citizenship. They are citizens of the United States (if they are born in the United States or to a U.S. citizen living outside the United States), and they are citizens of their tribal nations. As citizens of the United States, American Indians—like all other citizens—enjoy all the rights guaranteed in the Constitution, including freedom of speech, religion, and the press.

United States citizenship for America's original inhabitants was a long time coming. It is one of history's great ironies that American Indians—the first peoples of North America—were not guaranteed U.S. citizenship until 1924. Although two-thirds of Indian people (women who married U.S. citizens, for example) had gained citizenship through piecemeal laws enacted during the previous fifty years, American Indians were the last group in the United States to enjoy citizenship as a birthright. Charles Curtis (Kaw/Osage, 1860–1936), the first American Indian U.S. senator and later the vice president under Herbert Hoover, sponsored the Indian Citizenship Act while he was serving as the chairman of the Senate Committee on Indian Affairs. Congress supported the law as an extension of the government's assimilation policy. Some twelve thousand American Indians had served in the U.S. military during World War I, thus demonstrating, the thinking went, their ability to assimilate into white society.

Some traditional American Indian peoples do not embrace American citizenship, believing it interferes with tribal status as sovereign nations. Some tribes, such as the Haudenosaunee (Iroquois), have in the past issued their own passports. The 1924 act, however, grants

U.S. citizenship to American Indian peoples regardless of individual personal and political beliefs.

Citizenship for American Indian peoples did not automatically mean the right to vote in the individual states in which they resided. Like African Americans living in the southern states, American Indians faced oppression, racism, and discrimination, particularly when it came to voting rights. Discrimination was expressed most openly in the states with large Native populations, including Alaska, Arizona, Colorado, New Mexico, and Utah. American Indians could not vote in New Mexico until 1948; in Arizona, not until 1964. In South Dakota, Indian people were still fighting for the right to vote in county elections well into the mid-1970s.

Suzanne Evans, of the University of California, Berkeley, writes in the *Encyclopedia of North American Indians* (1996), "The right to vote is arguably the most significant characteristic of American citizenship. . . . But, despite its significance, the franchise has been denied to many groups throughout history, including blacks, women, and Indians. However, whereas blacks were formally enfranchised with the Fifteenth Amendment (1870) and women with the Nineteenth Amendment (1920), Indians cannot claim one defining historical moment when their right to vote was constitutionally secured."

—LIZ HILL AND NEMA MAGOVERN

POPULAR
MYTHS

How did some tribes get a reputation as warlike and others as peaceful?

Historically, most peoples, when confronted with newcomers who encroached on their lands, stole their food sources, and threatened their families with destruction and death, have sought to protect their lands and loved ones. In general the indigenous peoples of North and South America have been no exception. Of course, what appears to be common sense was not the case during the first visits of Europeans to the Western Hemisphere. Initially, a number of Native societies considered light-skinned Europeans to be gods worthy of veneration and even worship and welcomed them with great hospitality.

Typically, first encounters between Indians and Europeans were peaceful, but conflicts would soon develop, and non-Indians would characterize the formerly "peaceful" Indian communities as "warlike." Newcomers stereotyped Taíno and other Caribbean societies—some of the first people whom the Spanish encountered in the late 1400s and early 1500s—as peaceful because they did not immediately attack. Such was also the case when Captain James Cook landed in the Hawaiian Islands in 1778. Cook, believed to be the Hawaiian god Lono—who, it had been predicted, would return on a "floating island"—was warmly received by Native Hawaiians during his first and second visits to their lands. The enthusiastic greeting with which Native Hawaiians met Captain Cook and his crew was unusual, because the Native Hawaiians were known historically as a fierce and warlike people. Their friendly attitude quickly changed, however, during the second sojourn. In a dispute over stolen property, a fight among Native Hawaiians and Cook's men ensued, and Hawaiian warriors killed Cook on February 14, 1779, on the beach at Kealakekua Bay on the Big Island.

The Wampanoag people, who were present at the feast that is

commonly known as the first Thanksgiving, also treated the English settlers peacefully. As English hunger for land increased, however, the Wampanoag attitude also changed, culminating in King Philip's War of 1675–1676. This war between Native communities in the Northeast and British settlers proved devastating to the Native peoples. The conflict abrogated the original truce negotiated between the Wampanoag leader, Massasoit, and the governor of the Plymouth Colony.

Tribes also could gain reputations for being warlike or peaceful from neighboring tribes with whom they came into conflict. *Apache*, a word derived from the Zuni language, is translated to mean "enemy" or "fighting men." Apaches were known for their warlike stances toward other tribes and white settlers—although their reputation has perhaps been much exaggerated by the general hostility toward Native peoples. The Maya and Aztec peoples of Mesoamerica, whose civilizations flourished between approximately AD 250 and AD 1550, also were known initially for their warlike practices.

—LIZ HILL

WHY DO SOME PEOPLE THINK INDIANS DO NOT LAUGH OR SMILE?

Humor has always been an aspect of Native life, binding families and communities, regulating social behavior, and providing a release in times of strife. It is also a doorway to understanding, an "in" to the subtle nuances of a culture. Early European explorers and settlers, however, had no real interest in understanding the indigenous peoples of the "New World." To them Native people were incapable of complex thought and emotion, much less an intricate combination of the two such as humor.

Humor holds a revered place among Native people. The Trickster—Coyote, Raven, or Rabbit, for example—is an integral figure in Native lore. He is the lesson bearer who travels between the sacred and the profane, the spirit and the human world, and he often finds himself in humorous situations in which he creates and destroys to make the world what it is. Humor is often used to reinforce the social norms of the tribal or family group. Teasing is the preferred method. According to Kenneth Lincoln in *Indi'n Humor* (1993), the Hopi word for clowning means "to make a point." The *tsukuwimkya*, sacred clowns of the Hopi, and the *heyoka*, ritual clowns of the Lakota, behave contrary to accepted behavior to demonstrate the proper way to behave. They bathe with mud, stand on their heads, and laugh when they should cry. Their lessons go beyond basic social control, however. They illustrate the dual nature of life—the dark and the light, the suffering and the joyous.

The stoic image of the Indian has followed Native people for centuries, reaching its zenith during the age of still photography and the Hollywood Indian. Rarely does one find the smiling face of an Indian among the hundreds of photographs taken in the late 1800s

and early 1900s. Many of these photos were staged to fit the stereo-types of the photographer and his audience: the Native subjects were given traditional dress to wear (even if it was not from their culture) and posed with muted stares. Edward S. Curtis was among the most famous of these manipulators. Were the subjects of his photos longing for a simpler time or crying silently for their vanishing people? In truth, many were clamped from behind to keep them perfectly still, and the photography session included an explosive flash. Since many could not speak or understand English, the process could be traumatic. Many photographs were also taken just after tribal leaders had signed unfair treaties or Native prisoners had been captured by government forces.

These stone-faced portrayals carried over to the big and small screen in the figure of the grunting, broken-English-speaking nem-esis of the western cowboy. Even in more contemporary times we can find the stoic stereotype in characters such as Magua, in *The Last of the Mohicans* (1992), or Kocoum, Pocahontas's Native love interest in the Disney version of the myth (1995). Recently, Native writers and directors have been able to introduce audiences to the richness of Native humor, and even to a few insider jokes. *Smoke Signals* (1998) uses humor to subtly point out insidious movie stereo-types. Kate Montgomery, a non-Native director, wrote a romantic comedy titled *Christmas in the Clouds* (2001) to reflect the outlook of her funny, jovial, life-loving Native friends and acquaintances.

Native stand-up comedians, such as Charlie Hill (Oneida), An-drew Lacapa (Apache/Hopi/Tewa), and Don Burnstick (Cree), express Native humor in its most in-your-face form. The comics address every-thing from "rez" life to the expectations of the dominant culture to religion and spirituality. In the Trickster tradition, everything and nothing are sacred. Humor is medicine. Both Lacapa and Burnstick turned to humor and comedy as a way to deal with their scarred pasts. They see it as a way of healing and bringing people together. We can-not hurt one another if we are all laughing—at ourselves, each other, and the crazy world around us.

—ARWEN NUTTALL

WHO IS ON THE INDIAN NICKEL? WHAT IS THE INDIAN NICKEL?

In 1911 the sculptor James Earle Fraser was asked to design a replacement for the Liberty Head nickel. Fraser's goal was to create a coin that could not be confused with the currency of any other country, one that truly symbolized America. Fraser remarked, "I found no motif . . . so distinctive as the American buffalo, or bison. With the Indian head on the obverse, we have perfect unity in theme. It . . . is in line with the best traditions of coin design, where the purpose is to memorialize a nation or a people." The coin was a success, and Fraser and the U.S. Treasury Department received many letters from people who wanted to know the identity of the Indian.

Actually, the profile is a composite of three Plains Indians: Iron Tail (Sioux), Big Tree (Kiowa), and Two Moons (Cheyenne). On a visit to President Theodore Roosevelt, the men had stopped in New York, where Fraser sketched and photographed them. Unfortunately, the Indian nickel was replaced only twenty-five years later by a nickel with the buffalo still in place but the profile of Thomas Jefferson on the "heads" side of the coin.

As for the buffalo, Fraser said:

He was not a Plains buffalo but none other than Black Diamond, the contrariest animal in the Bronx Park Zoo. I stood for hours . . . catching his form and mood in plastic clay. Black Diamond was less conscious of the honor being conferred on him than of the annoyance which he suffered from insistent gazing. He refused point-blank to permit me to get side views of him and stubbornly showed his front face most of the time.

Rob Atkins. Close-up of the U.S. Indian head
nickel, ca. 2004.

© Getty Images.

The Indian nickel was issued on March 4, 1913. Coins from the
first bag of nickels ever produced were presented to President William H. Taft and thirty-three Indian chiefs at the groundbreaking
ceremonies for the National American Indian Memorial at Fort Wads-
worth, New York. By 1938, the year the coin was retired, more than
1.2 billion Indian nickels had been in circulation.

—MARY AHENAKEW

WAS TONTO A REAL INDIAN?

When *The Lone Ranger* hit the radio waves in 1933, audiences of all ages could feel the drama. Even without visual cues, it was easy for listeners to picture the characters. The advent of television in the late 1940s reinforced what had been imagined. The Lone Ranger was white, self-assured, quick to act, and gave orders like a field marshal, while Tonto, his submissive Indian sidekick, loyally followed instructions. Tonto and the Lone Ranger projected the personalities and images expected of them.

The character of Tonto marked a decisive break with the literary and cinematic stereotype of Indians as bloodthirsty savages forever on the warpath. Although Tonto was just as one-dimensional as his movie predecessors, he was a peaceful, dutiful, loyal pal who spoke pidgin English and wore clothes—headbands, feathers, fringed leather, moccasins—that could only belong to an Indian. This stereotype pervaded movie and television westerns of the 1950s and 1960s, remaining unchanged even when the actor playing it was not Native American.

Jay Silverheels (Mohawk), the most famous of several actors who played Tonto, was born Harry Smith in 1912 on the Six Nations Indian Reserve in Ontario, Canada. He played the role in the long-running *Lone Ranger* television series (1949–1957) as well as in two feature-length films. Silverheels's acting career began as a stuntman in 1937. After serving in World War II he played lacrosse and boxed. As an athlete, he adopted the last name "Silverheels." Having had a taste of acting, he set his sights on Hollywood and, as fortune would have it, he and Clayton Moore worked together before their long association as Tonto and the Lone Ranger. In 1949, while appearing

Tonto (Jay Silverheels [Mohawk]) and the Lone Ranger (Clayton Moore) hard at work in their familiar television show, ca. 1949–1957.

© Bettmann/CORBIS.

with Gene Autry in the film *The Cowboy and the Indians*, they caught a producer's attention. From this meeting came *The Lone Ranger* series, in which Silverheels became the first American Indian to play an American Indian on television.

In later years Silverheels became a spokesperson for Indian rights. He was opposed to having non-Indians playing Indian roles, and he became a respected teacher within the Indian acting community. He appeared on talk shows and variety shows. It is said that when he went on *The Tonight Show*, the audience was in stitches after he told Johnny Carson he had married an Italian woman to get even with Columbus. At the age of sixty-seven, he suffered a stroke, and succumbed on March 5, 1980. His ashes were buried at the Six Nations Indian Reserve.

However stereotypical Tonto may have been, the actor who played him ultimately opened doors of opportunity for future American Indian actors. Many American Indians today have played historical Indian figures, and many land dramatic roles that rely solely on their ability to bring a complex, multidimensional character to life on the screen. Harry Smith/Jay Silverheels had a long and successful career in Hollywood in many roles. He will be remembered, however, for the role he brought to life and legend, Tonto.

—RICO NEWMAN

Why Did Carved Wooden Indians Stand Outside Cigar Stores?

The stereotyping of ethnic groups has always been a part of American culture. Stereotypes are harmful because they reduce complex human beings to mere caricatures who are then ridiculed as inferior. American Indians have been stereotyped continuously ever since the first Europeans wrote and illustrated their accounts of the "New World." Beginning with these early, often-inaccurate depictions, Europeans have cultivated an intense fascination for Native peoples.

For centuries the cigar-store Indian has illustrated prevailing stereotypes. Made of carved wood or cast iron, the nearly life-sized statues of Native Americans can be found today in antiques and "western" shops around the United States. Their original location, however, was outside tobacco and smoke shops.

Why was this depiction of a Native American an appropriate way to announce to the public the location of a smoke shop? The answer is quite simple. Tobacco was a plant first cultivated by the Native peoples of the Americas thousands of years ago. Europeans got their first taste of it when Christopher Columbus accepted it from the Taíno people three days after he made landfall in the Americas in 1492. From that time on tobacco and the New World's Native peoples were connected.

Cigar-store Indians appeared as early as the 1600s in Europe. In those days much of the general population was illiterate, so advertising to reach the masses was most easily accomplished through the use of visual images. American Indians and tobacco was a connection that many people—Europeans and, later, Americans—could understand; thus, the popular use of Native figures outside smoke shops.

From the time of their first encounters, Europeans have tended to romanticize Native peoples, and one sees that romanticism in some

Wooden statue of an American Indian man in front of a New York cigar, book, and novelty shop, ca. 1895.

© Bettmann/CORBIS.

of the earliest cigar-store Indians. The majority of the European public had never actually seen an Indian person face-to-face; what they knew of American Indians was from explorers' illustrations. Some of the early cigar-store Indians looked more like African enslaved peoples than they did indigenous Americans. Figures depicting Native females were extremely popular, and some of the woman figures included Indian infants. Later, the carved figures looked more like the Native peoples of the Great Plains, replete with feathered war bonnets and the clothing common among those tribes.

Although cigar-store Indians are rarely seen today outside cigar and smoke shops (their presence declined in the late nineteenth century owing to increased restrictions on the use of sidewalk space), they are still manufactured. Many sources for purchasing cigar-store Indians can be found on the Internet, proving that antique—and newly made—cigar-store Indians remain highly collectible pieces of Americana.

—LIZ HILL

DID INDIANS REALLY USE SMOKE SIGNALS? DO THEY TODAY?

Yes. Some Native peoples living on the Great Plains and in the Southwest used smoke signals hundreds of years ago. For example, the Navajo and Apache transmitted smoke signals as a military tactic to warn of the approach of enemies. But the use of smoke to convey messages has been greatly exaggerated—and even ridiculed—in twentieth- and twenty-first-century mainstream popular culture, particularly in Hollywood movies, advertisements, and cartoons.

The image is now deeply ingrained in the public consciousness. Think of it: a Native man, dressed in the style of the Great Plains cultures, long hair in braids with a headband and feather, sits on the edge of a cliff (of course in the "Indian style," with his legs crossed in front of him). The Indian man is fanning a fire with a blanket, from which smoke billows upward. His smoke "signals" are received and interpreted by another Native man, perhaps miles away.

American popular culture also has distorted the rudimentary character of smoke signals and would have the average person believing that an entire language has been built around their use. Native peoples did not use smoke to spell out entire words, as is often depicted in the media. Neither did all tribes use smoke to communicate.

Today, when someone mentions smoke signals, the image of an Indian immediately comes to mind. When asked by *Cineaste* magazine about the title of his film *Smoke Signals* (1998), author Sherman Alexie (Spokane/Coeur d'Alene) said, "On the surface, it's a stereotypical title; you think of Indians in blankets on the plains sending smoke signals, so it brings up a stereotypical image that's vaguely humorous. But people will also instantly recognize that this is about Indians."

Indian people no longer use smoke signals as a mode of communication. News and information that travel from one Native American person to another—and to others around the country—are sometimes said jokingly to travel on the "moccasin telegraph" (or, in the case of Native Hawaiians, on the "coconut wireless"), which is a way of acknowledging the speed at which news travels to Native communities no matter how far apart they are located.

Today's Native peoples communicate by written messages, telephone, fax, cell phone, and email.

—LIZ HILL

WHAT DO INDIANS DO FOR THANKSGIVING?

The Thanksgiving Day feast that is celebrated in the United States first took place over three days sometime between September 20 and November 9, 1621, among the settlers of Plymouth Colony (in Massachusetts) and approximately ninety Native people of the Wampanoag Nation. Contrary to popular myth, the Pilgrim/Wampanoag gathering was probably not the first public feast of thanksgiving held by the English in the "New World," but rather was one of approximately three that had likely occurred since 1610, most notably at the Jamestown Colony. It is the Pilgrim/Wampanoag story of the "first" Thanksgiving, however, that has been passed down to generations of schoolchildren as a time-honored part of American history.

Perhaps the most enduring part of the first Thanksgiving myth is that the Pilgrims hosted the feast for the Native people present. The reality is that after a cautious approach on the part of the Wampanoag, both groups contributed to the feast. Without Wampanoag agricultural expertise, however, the English would not have survived to celebrate their first Thanksgiving. Unaccustomed to the extreme weather conditions of New England and without enough food, warm clothing, or other provisions to see them through the particularly harsh winter of 1620–1621, the Pilgrims had quickly become destitute and were on the verge of starvation. On the other hand, the Wampanoag people—members of one of the most powerful confederacies of Native nations of the time—had plenty of food, some of which the English stole to survive. It is both ironic and tragic that the Wampanoag Nation in the coming years would suffer an almost complete decimation of their once-enormous numbers, power, and influence—at the hands of the same people whose survival they had helped ensure.

"We're here to escape religious persecution.
What are you here for?"

In 1863, during the depths of the Civil War, Abraham Lincoln proclaimed that a day be set aside to give thanks publicly for life's bounty. Today, Thanksgiving is a national holiday in both the United States and Canada (in the United States on the fourth Thursday in November, and in Canada on the second Monday in October). Most Native people observe the holiday alongside everyone else, with the foods that have become traditional Thanksgiving staples, such as turkey (which was documented as one of the foods served at the feast in 1621) and stuffing. Indian people also use Thanksgiving as a time to get together with family and friends.

The idea of reserving just one day to give thanks for food, shelter, and the blessings of a healthy life is alien to many Native cultures, however. Most Indian people, even today, say that they give thanks each day for the bounty in their lives. It is customary for people in many Native cultures of the Western Hemisphere to greet each day with special prayers of thanksgiving and to give thanks at various times, including at harvest festivals and ceremonies, throughout the year.

On Thanksgiving Day, while most Native people are sitting down to turkey dinners, some prefer to observe the day as one of mourning—for what happened to the millions of Indians who lived on the North and South American continents before the arrival of the Europeans.

—LIZ HILL

DID ALASKA NATIVES REALLY ABANDON ELDERLY PEOPLE ON ICE FLOES TO DIE?

There are many different Native groups in Alaska and the subarctic. Because the geographic diversity of the region is immense, some groups experienced hardship in their daily lives more often than others, especially those living farthest north. It is among these groups that stories about leaving injured members and elders to fend for themselves are most often told.

Leaving elders behind was not routinely practiced, and it was not a universal custom for Native peoples. It did happen, however, during severe winters marked by massive shortages of food and supplies. As contact with Europeans became more frequent, both the practice and the stories about it subsided. The last recorded instance occurred in 1939, but it was rare long before then.

Respect and caring for elders is important to Natives in general. Even when food was low and groups were burdened and weakened, making the choice to leave a family member behind was painful. In the interest of preserving itself, the group would focus on caring for its hunters and other contributing adults, and its young people—those who could provide food and a future. It was awareness of what would preserve the group that sometimes prompted an elder to instruct the group to leave him or her behind at a camp.

The practice of leaving elders behind is addressed by Velma Wallis (Gwich'in) in her book *Two Old Women* (1993). Because of the seemingly cruel nature of the practice, Wallis's book was at first harshly criticized by her European-American critics and counterparts. Cultural sensitivity has brought different world views to the forefront in recent years, helping the rest of the world understand how an elder could be left to die in the woods or, if near water, on an ice floe.

—MIRANDA BELARDE-LEWIS

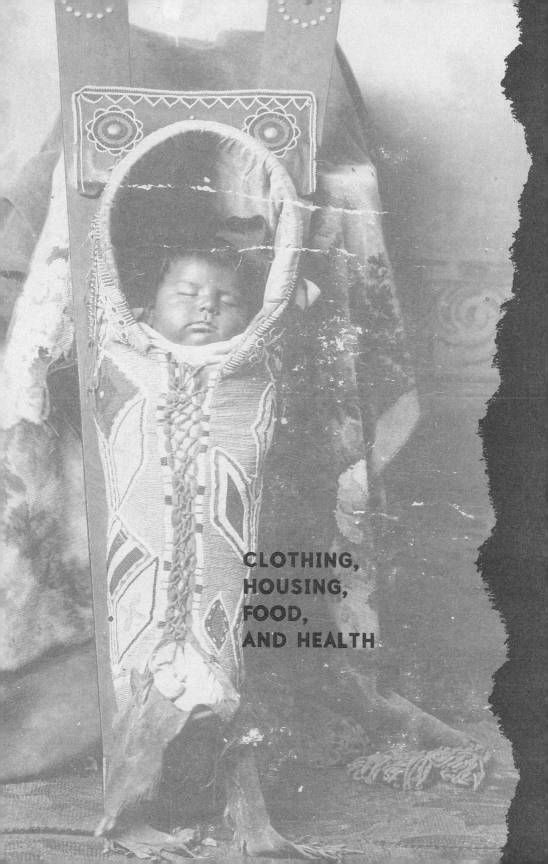

CLOTHING,
HOUSING,
FOOD,
AND HEALTH

Do all Indians live in tipis?

Most American Indians live in contemporary homes, apartments, condos, and co-ops, just like every other citizen of the twenty-first century. Some Native people who live in modern homes do erect and use tipis in the summer for ceremonies and other community events. But most Indians in the Americas, even those who live in their community's traditional dwellings, have never used tipis at all.

Tipis are the traditional homes of Plains Indians, but in other regions of the Western Hemisphere Native people lived in many different kinds of dwellings. Whether a tribe lived in a buffalo-hide tipi, an adobe hogan (dwellings made of adobe and supported by rocks or timbers), a birch-bark wigwam, or an igloo made of ice, the home's structure and materials were suited to each tribe's needs and environment. Some Diné (Navajo) people, for example, still live in hogans because the structures are well adapted to the desert, which can be extremely hot during the day and cold at night. During the day the hogan remains cool inside as the adobe absorbs the sun's heat. At night the structure releases the heat, keeping everyone inside comfortable.

The Great Plains at one time sustained millions of buffalo, and the Plains Indians depended almost entirely on the buffalo for their basic needs—including shelter. Their larger tipis were each made of as many as eighteen buffalo hides. Pueblo people of the Southwest live in homes made of adobe, which were the first apartment-style structures in North America.

American Indians have traditionally lived in structures that took best advantage of their individual resources, environment, and location. Inuit people constructed domed structures called igloos, which

George Haywood.
An Indian Village of the
Manhattans, for *D. T.
Valentine's Manual, 1858.*

Original engraving courtesy
of the Museum of the City of
New York. Postcard
version ca. 1910.

were made from blocks of snow. The coastal Inuit used igloos as temporary hunting shelters, but the interior Inuit lived in them year-round. An igloo could be built in about an hour and easily repaired or replaced. They are still used as temporary hunting shelters.

The people of the Haudenosaunee (Iroquois) Confederacy built longhouses made from logs, saplings, and bark, all of which were abundant in their forested environment. Each longhouse could shelter several families and, if needed, could be expanded to accommodate more people. During World War II, when U.S. troops needed inexpensive and easily constructed housing, military architects modeled what came to be known as Quonset huts on the longhouse design. Today not only longhouses but also many other traditional Native dwellings are used primarily as places for social and ceremonial gatherings.

—STEPHANIE BETANCOURT

What Kinds of Foods Do Indians Eat?

Who hasn't experienced the enticing smell of popcorn upon entering a movie theater or enjoyed a big bowl of potato chips and guacamole while watching the Super Bowl game? These are just a few of the sumptuous foods that have their origins among Native Americans of the Western Hemisphere. At the top of the long list of plants grown or processed by American Indians are corn, beans, squashes, pumpkins, peppers, potatoes, sweet potatoes, tomatoes, peanuts, wild rice, chocolate, pineapple, avocado, papaya, pecans, strawberries, blueberries, cranberries, and sunflowers. More than half the crops grown worldwide today were initially cultivated in the Americas.

American Indians hunted, herded, cultivated, and gathered a vast variety of species. The sciences of plant cultivation and food preparation were highly developed in the pre-Columbian Americas. By the time of the Spanish invasion in 1492, Indians in the Andes had developed more than a thousand different species of potato, each of which thrived in distinct growing conditions. Native Americans throughout the hemisphere developed at least as many varieties of corn to suit climates ranging from the northern woodland areas to the tropics. Today corn grows over a larger area than does any other cultivated food in the world.

The people of northeastern North America were among those who recognized the symbiotic relationship between corn, beans, and squashes: the bean climbs the natural trellis of the corn stalk, while the squash shades the ground below, discouraging other plants from spreading and choking the corn roots. Each plant also gives and takes different nutrients from the soil. The people of the Iroquois Confed-

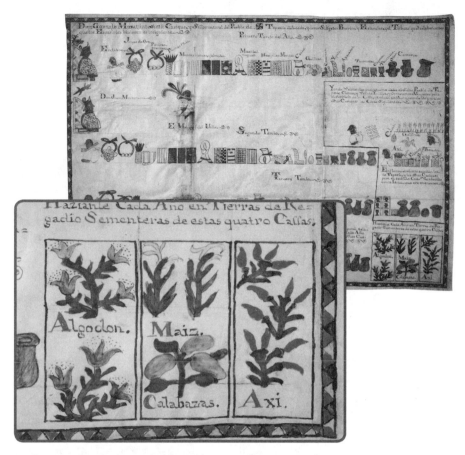

A record of tribute paid by Native people to Spanish overlords. Items pictured include slaves, gold, precious stones, fine feathers, textiles, cacao, chickens, sandals, woven chairs, rattles, gourd vessels, bowls, pots, and pitchers. A detail from the painting shows some of the principal crops grown by Native people in the region: cotton, corn, squash, and peppers.

Painted tribute record of Tepexi de la Seda,
18th c. copy of ca. 16th c. original. Puebla, Mexico. 8/4482

eracy called these crops the Three Sisters, or the sustainers, because of their importance to the well-being and survival of the people.

Many foods and food techniques have changed little from those developed by Native people. Modern manufacturers ferment, dry, and roast cacao beans to extract chocolate in much the same way as did Maya and Aztec growers. Along the North Pacific Coast, salmon is dried and smoked using processes that have existed for millennia. On the Great Plains, buffalo was the fundamental food source—entire cultures developed around communal buffalo hunts. Today Native breeding programs are restoring buffalo populations, making the meat available as a healthy alternative to beef.

Since reservations were first established in the late nineteenth century, many American Indians have depended on nontraditional, government-issued food commodities, from which has arisen one of the most delicious and least healthful "Native" foods: fry bread. Made with flour, yeast, and lard, fry bread is served warm with powdered sugar or syrup, or loaded with meat, cheese, shredded lettuce, and tomato to make another familiar treat: the Navajo (or "Indian") taco.

Most Native people today eat the foods that other Americans do, but traditional foods such as salmon, venison, wild strawberries, varieties of beans and chilies, and especially corn remain integral to seasonal ceremonies, dances, and other special occasions throughout Indian Country. Increased nationwide interest in fresh, local foods has led to renewed cultivation of indigenous ingredients and the creation of nontraditional dishes that bring out their flavor.

So, when you dig into a bowl of chili, a pile of mashed potatoes, or a piece of pumpkin pie, remember that such seemingly modern dishes depend on ingredients that were first cultivated, cooked, and given to the world by Native Americans.

—STEPHANIE BETANCOURT

Before Contact with Europeans, Did Indians Make All Their Clothing from Animal Skins?

No, not all clothing was made of animal skins, furs, or other animal parts. Many American Indians made their clothing from plant materials, including cotton and yucca, and from wool. Between 3500 BC and 2300 BC, Native people in Mesoamerica and on the eastern slope of the Peruvian Andes domesticated many varieties of cotton, a plant that is indigenous to the Western Hemisphere. Archaeologists have found seven- to eight-thousand-year-old mummies wrapped in cotton textiles, and it is possible that wild cotton was used for clothing in Peru as early as 10,000 BC. American Indians in southwestern North America began growing cotton shortly after 1500 BC, and the earliest textile found in present-day New Mexico dates back to AD 700. As early as AD 300, ancestral Puebloans were gathering other plant fibers, such as yucca, willow, and juniper bark, processing them, and weaving them into sandals, blankets, leggings, socks, belts, and other articles of clothing.

Today, Native people wear all kinds of modern attire, just like everyone else. Almost all tribes, however, continue to wear traditional and dance clothing, which is customary for social and ceremonial occasions. Ceremonial wear is made of modern textiles in addition to other materials—including animal skins—that predate the arrival of Europeans.

—MARY AHENAKEW

Kenneth Garrett. Maya Indians in the highlands
of Guatemala dressed in jeans and traditionally
patterned clothing.

© National Geographic Collection/Getty Images.

DID INDIANS WEAR SOCKS?

Yes, some Native peoples wore socks. In general, Native people who made their homes in warmer climates and in places such as the Hawaiian Islands, California, and the Northwest Coast (where people spent a lot of time near the ocean, fishing and gathering food), went barefoot most of the time. Still, many tribal peoples wore some type of protective footgear to shield their feet from, for example, the hot and inhospitable ground of the desert or swampy ground in southeastern North America. Most did not wear stockings or socks, opting only for the footgear. But, especially in the colder climates, Native peoples wore socks inside moccasins or boots to add an extra layer of warmth.

Native Americans ingeniously constructed socks from natural materials that could be found locally, including the skins of muskrats, rabbits, caribou, moose, ducks, badgers, and many other animals. Socks also were made from mountain-sheep wool or woven from a variety of plants—including yucca, dune grass, and many other types of local plants and grasses—depending on availability. Some people, such as the Pueblo of the Southwest, knitted or crocheted their socks from cotton yarn.

Native peoples who wore socks made of animal skins include the Northern Paiutes (Nevada, Oregon, California), whose socks were fashioned of badger and rabbit skin in the winter, and the Southern Paiutes (Nevada, Utah, California), who wore form-fitting socks of badger and squirrel skins that looked like mittens. The Mi'kmaq, whose ancestral lands stretch from northern Maine into southeastern Canada, wore socks made from the skins of muskrats, rabbits, or woodchucks, and the Beothuk people of Newfoundland made stockings

from rabbit fur or grass. Western Cree socks were made of rabbit and caribou, with the fur of the animals placed on the inside of the socks for additional protection from the elements. In general, the peoples of the subarctic made their socks from caribou, rabbits, and moose, fashioning them into pouches that fit the foot. The Aleuts and Yup'iks of southwestern Alaska wove socks of dune or other grass, and the Native peoples of Alaska's far north also used polar bear fur.

—LIZ HILL

DO NATIVE AMERICAN PARENTS STILL PUT THEIR BABIES IN CRADLEBOARDS? ARE THE CRADLEBOARDS COMFORTABLE?

Yes. Many Native people still use cradleboards to secure their babies. While they may not be as pervasive as they were, say, two hundred years ago, you can still see children all over Indian Country wrapped in blankets and packed in their cradleboards. The cradleboards reflect a wide variety of tribal styles, and the materials used to make them range from wood, buckskin, and plant fibers to canvas and other fabrics. Most cradleboards have a protective arch above the child's head, which is made from a willow branch, reeds, or carved wood.

Traditionally, cradleboards were highly utilitarian; a child could be carried on his or her mother's back by a strap attached to the back of the cradleboard. The strap went across the mother's upper chest and upper arms or across her forehead. This arrangement freed the mother's hands to work. The cradleboard could also be hung or propped up so that the mother and other family members had visual contact with the baby.

The Haudenosaunee (Iroquois) people of the Northeast have always made cradleboards from wood and have carved beautiful designs on the backboards and protective wooden arches. They sometimes add paintings to enhance the carvings. Cradleboards made by many of the Plains tribes have wooden frames covered with soft buckskin and elaborately decorated with glass beads and porcupine quills. Other materials used in decoration are sequins, shells, silk- or cotton-thread embroidery, satin ribbon, metal tacks, and horsehair.

Some designs include sacred symbols and colors to bring the child good fortune and long life. Parents in many tribes saved the child's umbilical cord, which was made into an amulet, carried on the cradleboard

A Comanche baby in a cradleboard, 1895. Fort Sill, Oklahoma.

P13191

as a toy, and kept throughout the person's life. The Western Shoshone had two types of cradleboards made of woven willow reeds: the boat basket, which was used for newborns, and the hoop basket, used once the baby's neck muscles were strong enough to hold up his or her head. A woven willow shade was added to the basket to protect the baby from the sun and keep the cradle upright if accidentally bumped. Some tribes, such as the Pomo of present-day California, used a sitting-style cradleboard, designed so that the child's legs hung over the bottom edge. Today many of the woven cradleboards are covered with cloth, which is cool and also washable.

The cradleboard protects the infant physically and emotionally, allowing the baby to feel secure. Some cradleboards have bindings that attach the child directly to the backboard; other styles have a sack attached. The sacks (some tribes call them moss sacks because moss was used as a diapering material years ago) have binding along the bias to secure the infant. Some people use only the moss sacks, without a backboard. The flat back of the cradleboard keeps the infant's spine aligned, and the binding helps strengthen the baby's muscles by creating resistance when the baby pushes against it. Some types of cradleboards include additional cushions and supports for the crown of the head, neck, and feet. Most babies stay in cradleboards until they can walk and/or work their way out of them. A lot of time and effort is put into making a cradleboard, and its aesthetic beauty reflects the deep love parents and families have for their children.

—MARY AHENAKEW

DO NATIVE AMERICAN PARENTS STILL PUT THEIR BABIES IN CRADLEBOARDS?

89

How did Pendleton Blankets Become So Important to American Indians?

At many Native American powwows, giveaways, graduations, and ceremonies, brilliantly patterned woolen Pendleton blankets are given away, wrapped around the shoulders of individuals to honor them for their achievements or contributions. Prized for their beauty, bold colors, and intricate designs, Pendleton blankets have been used in many ways by Native people since they first encountered them in the early 1900s.

Before Europeans made contact with tribes in North America, Native people made blankets by sewing together buffalo hides or the pelts of small animals, as well as by weaving wool, feathers, down, or mountain-goat hair into coverings, or robes. After Europeans arrived and began trading with Native communities, woolen blankets—known widely as "Indian trading blankets"—became popular and gained in value. The woolen blankets were especially prized in the damp northern climate for their ability to stay warm even when wet. Early trading blankets, such as those made by the Hudson's Bay Company beginning in the late 1600s, were woven in simple plaid and block designs. These gave way in the 1700s to brighter, more complex patterns as more weaving mills were established. Even more sophisticated weaving techniques and influences were imported from France in the mid-1800s.

In 1895, Pendleton Woolen Mills in Portland, Oregon, began manufacturing bed blankets and robes especially for American Indians. The company's first catalog, published in 1901, featured a photograph of Chief Joseph (1840–1904), the renowned leader of the Nez Perce tribe, draped in a Pendleton robe. In 1909 the owners rebuilt and expanded their mill, and they began working directly with tribes

Famed for his 1877 surrender speech after helping to lead
his Nez Perce band on a fourteen-hundred-mile tactical
retreat from northeastern Oregon toward the Canadian
border, Chief Joseph continued to speak eloquently for the
rest of his life against the injustice of United States policy
toward his people.

Major Lee Moorhouse. Chief Joseph (Nez Perce, 1840–
1904) wrapped in a Pendleton blanket, ca. 1901.

Courtesy of Pendleton Woolen Mills.

in eastern Oregon and the Southwest. They set out to learn more about the colors, symbols, and designs that Native communities valued, so they could produce blankets that specifically appealed to tribes in these regions.

Trade blankets featuring bold new patterns soon made their way throughout the Southwest, and they were quickly adopted for everyday and ceremonial uses, often replacing hide robes and handwoven textiles. Handed out at powwows, giveaways, and Northwest Coast potlatch ceremonies, the blankets soon became symbols of wealth and forms of currency. As Pendleton trade blankets grew in popularity, they became an important part of Native people's lives—given to young women as part of a dowry, worn or given away on special occasions, or used in the home. Presented to honor others, Pendleton blankets also were collected for one's own family, to be handed down to the next generation.

Today Native peoples still value Pendleton blankets and use them in important ceremonies. In everyday life blankets are used as sturdy floor or wall coverings, or for practical purposes such as cushioning a horse saddle, car seat, or baby cradle. Known as Pendleton's "first customers," Native Americans have deeply rooted traditions tied to the giving and receiving of these blankets. For many, being wrapped in a Pendleton robe is to be enveloped in warmth, love, and admiration.

—TANYA THRASHER

ARE INDIANS MORE PRONE TO CERTAIN DISEASES THAN THE GENERAL POPULATION? WHY?

Statistics show that considerable health disparities exist between American Indians and the general population of the United States. With a life expectancy of 71.1 years of age, Indians live on average 4.7 years less than the rest of the nation. Poverty, unhealthy eating habits, inadequate housing, poor sanitation, uneven quality of and access to medical care, and resistance to seeking treatment all contribute to the current health peril.

Indians face grim statistics for most diseases, with rates that are 4.9 times higher for liver disease and cirrhosis, more than 7 times higher for death due to alcoholism, 3 times higher for accidental deaths, and more than 6 times higher for tuberculosis, a disease often thought to be a plague of the past. Although drastic differences between Indians and the general population are evident for most diseases, the gap narrows for the leading causes of death, which for both groups are cardiovascular disease and malignant tumors. If there is one disease that Native Americans are more prone to than the rest of the population, it is adult-onset diabetes, and it is presently a threat that looms large.

Type 2 diabetes is on the rise for all Americans but significantly so for Native Americans, who have seen a 93 percent increase within their population since 1981 and currently suffer a diabetes death rate that is 3.5 times greater than the rest of the nation. One of the most important factors increasing the risk of diabetes for anyone is unhealthy weight, and, unfortunately, 37 percent of Native Americans are overweight, while 15 percent are obese. Through European contact, federally issued commodity foodstuffs, and poverty, contemporary Indians have developed a diet that is substantially different from

that of their ancestors, one that often leads to the weight conditions conducive to diabetes.

The second critical factor that increases diabetes risk is genetics. Over centuries in a harsh and often unreliable land, Native Americans evolved metabolic genes that allowed them to efficiently store fat and survive famine. With the quantity and types of food available today, these genes are no longer beneficial. Nobody knows this better than the Tohono O'odham people of Arizona. Once a desert tribe whose meals were often few and far between, the Tohono O'odham now have the highest rates of diabetes in the world—approximately 50 percent of the tribe is afflicted. Ongoing medical research in the community is now establishing valuable knowledge about the genetic predisposition to diabetes. Meanwhile, the Tohono O'odham are joining tribes from across the country to actively confront the disease through diabetes prevention campaigns. As for all Americans and many other health concerns, regular exercise and a healthy diet are paramount in the battle against diabetes.

—JENNIFER ERDRICH

WHAT ARE THE RATES OF ALCOHOLISM, DRUG ADDICTION, AND SUICIDE AMONG AMERICAN INDIANS?

There is no doubt that alcohol abuse is a significant concern for Native American communities, but many misconceptions obscure the reality of this complicated situation. According to the most recent statistics published by Indian Health Services in *Trends in Indian Health, 1998–1999* the alcoholism death rate for American Indians and Alaska Natives is more than seven times the rate for the general population of the United States. In addition, alcohol is implicated in three-fourths of all traumatic American Indian deaths. It is a major factor in the high rates of suicide, homicide, automobile accidents, crime, family abuse, and fetal alcohol syndrome in Native American communities. These numbers, however, do little to explain the history, the present reality, and the confusion over American Indians and alcohol.

Researchers have proposed different theories about why alcoholism is still a scourge to the Native American population. Historical explanations describe how past laws making it illegal for Indians to possess or consume alcohol led to a consumption pattern of binge drinking. For those less inclined to historical arguments, many researchers have sought a genetic explanation for the disease. Some studies have focused on two candidate genes associated with alcohol metabolism that sometimes have a different form in American Indians. To date, no report has conclusively confirmed that the gene variants do indeed cause American Indians to process alcohol any differently than the rest of the population or cause them to be more prone to alcoholism. Scientific literature is careful to state that there *may* be a link, but that important qualification is often overlooked. Meanwhile, the idea of possible genetic susceptibility can be misconstrued into myths of "genetic weakness"

that misled both non-Indians and Indians themselves. Lost in the mythmaking is the fact that individual tolerance levels vary among individuals.

Amid the controversy and confusion, the risks and causes of alcoholism have yet to be clearly identified. Many focus on the critical role that socioeconomic, cultural, and psychological factors play in the disconcerting rates of Native American alcoholism. Poor education, alarming poverty, family and community instability, and low occupational status increase the prevalence of alcoholism in any family. Sadly, these conditions are all too real for many American Indians.

As for drug addiction and suicide, the rates are elevated in the Native American population as well. The drug-related death rate for American Indians and Alaska Natives is 65 percent higher than for the rest of the general population of the United States, while the suicide rate is 72 percent higher. Again, the historical and current causes of these perplexing and difficult situations must be considered just as seriously as the numbers themselves to better understand the existence of the disparities.

—JENNIFER ERDRICH

CEREMONY
AND RITUAL

DID ANCIENT MESOAMERICANS PRACTICE HUMAN SACRIFICE DURING THEIR BALL GAMES?

Mesoamerica includes the present-day countries of Mexico, Belize, Guatemala, Honduras, and El Salvador. Various games involving rubber balls, unique to that region but extending as far north as Arizona and east to the Caribbean, were played from approximately 1500 BC until the Spanish conquest three thousand years later. The Olmec people developed rubber from the sap of the *ulquahuitl*, or the rubber tree.

For the ancient Mesoamericans, the ball game was not merely a game by contemporary definitions, but rather a sacred rite practiced to maintain cosmic balance between life and death. It had symbolic associations with celestial movements—particularly those of the sun and moon—and with agricultural fertility. In addition, it served as a method of conflict resolution within and between communities, maintaining sociopolitical categories and replacing high-casualty warfare.

A description of the ball game as a ceremonial rite tied to celestial bodies and transformation through death and rebirth is found in the *Popol Vuh*, a Maya creation story. The Maya gods created humans in their present form, the first of whom were the skilled ballplayers Hun Hunahpu and Vucub Hunahpu. Their raucous ball playing so enrages the lords of the Underworld, the Xibalba, that they trick the brothers into playing a game in which they are killed and buried under the ball court.

The sons of Hun Hunahpu, known as the Hero Twins, grow up to become even more highly skilled ballplayers than their father and uncle, but their talents quickly get them into trouble with the Underworld lords. They are challenged by the lords of the Underworld to a ball game and a series of tests. The twins cut off their own heads and

yet come back to life, fooling the Xibalbas into not demanding as much death. Conquering the Xibalba lords, the Hero Twins disinter the bodies of their father and uncle, placing them in the heavens to become the sun and moon. Most important, the twins gain for human beings the right to replace the "heart" sacrifice with the ritual burning of the "heart" of *copal*, a sacred tree resin.

From this creation story, the Mesoamerican ball game can be seen primarily as a battle between the darkness and the light, the death of the sun as it enters the Underworld and its rebirth each morning as it ascends into the sky. The life-sustaining sun is intimately tied to the cycle of the seasons and, thus, agricultural fertility. Evidence suggests that some individuals were sacrificed upon the outcome of some Mesoamerican ball games but also points to a dynamic that led in a different spiritual direction.

—ARWEN NUTTALL

Is it True That White People Invented Scalping, or Did the Practice Originate with Native Americans?

While a few tribes took enemy scalps as trophies of war, many Native peoples considered the practice repugnant. But thanks to early frontier literature and, later, Hollywood westerns, the scalping has become part of the American Indian stereotype. Certainly the practice was not exclusive to American Indians. In the *Handbook of American Indians North of Mexico* (1959), Frederick Hodge states that the practice was noted among Scythians (Persian warriors who lived in the fifth century BC) as far back as the time of the Greek historian Herodotus. Archaeologists believe they have found evidence of scalping on pre-Columbian skulls in North America, at sites both east and west of the Mississippi.

Scalping by North American Indians was first recorded by Europeans in the mid-1500s. In the *Encyclopedia of North American Indians* (1996), historian James Axtell documents some of these encounters: "On his voyage up the St. Lawrence in 1535–36, Jacques Cartier was shown by the Stadaconans at Quebec 'the skins of five men's heads, stretched on hoops, like parchment.' In 1540, two of Hernando de Soto's men, the first Europeans to reach west Florida, were seized by Indians. The killers of one 'removed his head, or rather, all around his skull . . . and carried it off as evidence of their deed.'"

Europeans manipulated Indians by encouraging warfare between tribes, arming them with guns and knives through trade, and offering bounties to Indians for Indian scalps. The practice of scalping turned into the practice of murder during the 1600s, when English colonial governments began offering scalp bounties. Indian "enemies" were hunted and killed for their scalps, which became more valuable than beaver, otter, or any of the other animal pelts in demand at the

time. This systematic murder for profit spread westward with European settlement, continuing until about 1800.

In 1694 the first Massachusetts colonial proclamation to encourage volunteer hunters offered bounties "for every [hostile] Indian, great or small, which they shall kill, or take and bring prisoner." The act was renewed in 1704, but the General Court, deciding to follow a more "Christian practice," established a scale based on age and sex. Scalps of "men or youths capable of bearing armes" were worth one hundred pounds; women and children in their teen years and above were worth only ten pounds; and no reward was given for killing children under ten years old. Any captured children were instead sold as slaves and sent out of the colonies.

For colonial governments in North America, scalping appears to have been a favored technique, no matter who the supposed enemy. In 1688 the French governor of Canada became the first to encourage Indian scalping of whites. In his proclamation, ten beaver skins were offered to Indians in northern New England for every enemy scalp, "Christian or Indian." And in 1696 the New York Council resolved "for the future, that Six pounds shall be given to each Christian or Indian as a Reward who shall kill a French man or Indian Enemy."

—MARY AHENAKEW

DID ANY INDIANS PRACTICE CANNIBALISM?

Some Indian people apparently engaged in cannibalism—the eating of humans by other humans—as a part of their religious and cultural beliefs. In this, Native Americans were no exception among cultures worldwide. But, generally speaking, cannibalism was feared and abhorred by most Native people, much as it is today by Native and non-Native people everywhere in the world.

In his book *The Indian Heritage of America* (1968), Alvin Josephy Jr. offers a number of accounts of cannibalism, particularly among pre-Columbian tribes of Central and South America, including some of the peoples of the Caribbean region. In many cultures, such as the Maya and the Haudenosaunee (Iroquois), however, basic cultural teachings opposed cannibalism, creating a dynamic both for and against the practice. According to Josephy, cannibalism occurred, "here and there on both continents, although the reasons for its practice differed considerably among various tribes."

In his book *In the Hands of the Great Spirit: The 20,000-Year History of American Indians* (2003), Jake Page also takes up the issue of cannibalism. While not denying that some ritualistic cannibalism did take place among some groups, Page also notes the lack of evidence for most accounts of cannibalism: "European accounts of cannibalism among various groups of American Indians would accompany virtually all of the movements of Europeans into Indian territory, and the subject is (as can be imagined) one of the most emotionally laden in Indian history and, of course, one of the most painful to discuss in any context."

—LIZ HILL

WHAT DID INDIANS REALLY SMOKE IN THOSE PEACE PIPES?

Pipes and tobacco are sacred to Native peoples throughout North America. For American Indians, pipes are the instrument, or conduit, through which smoke and prayers are carried to the spirits. Each tribe has its own ceremonies and occasions for using pipes and tobacco.

Many Native people mix other dried plant materials with tobacco leaves. For example, the Chippewa add the dried inner bark of the dogwood tree to the tobacco mixture. The combination of tobacco and other ingredients is commonly called *kinnickinnick*, an Algonquian word of the Chippewa and Cree that means "what is mixed." There is also a plant that the Chippewa/Cree of Montana call *kinnikinnick*. Leaves of this plant are mixed with tobacco and act as a natural preservative to keep the tobacco fresh.

The two most abundant types of tobacco that grew in the Americas before contact with Europeans were *Nicotiana tabacum* in the Caribbean and South America and *Nicotiana rustica* in North America. By the first millennium AD, Native peoples had started cultivating them. In addition to being smoked, tobacco was used as a laxative, to dress wounds, and to relieve toothaches. The Maya of Central America and the Taíno of the Caribbean rolled tobacco in tobacco leaves to form cigars. The Aztec filled reeds with tobacco, creating an ancient version of a cigarette.

By the early 1600s the Spanish of the West Indies had imported the more fragrant *Nicotiana tabacum* to Europe, where it became wildly popular. The harsher *Nicotiana rustica* was introduced (along with the white potato) to England in 1586 by members of Sir Walter Raleigh's failed expedition to Virginia, but it was not until colonist

John Rolfe began experimenting with Caribbean tobacco seed in 1612 that the Virginia colony had a viable cash crop and a means of survival.

For European colonists, tobacco was a recreational pleasure and an economic mainstay. But for indigenous Americans, the plant has always played a more meaningful role. Integrated into Native cultures for millennia, tobacco leaves and tobacco smoke remain an important part of Native ceremonial life.

—MARY AHENAKEW

What is "Counting Coup"?

For the Sioux, Crow, Cheyenne, Mandan, and other Plains Indian groups, "counting coup" meant successfully challenging an enemy in one of four specific ways. Touching a live opponent, taking an enemy's weapon during face-to-face combat, capturing a tied horse from an opponent's camp, and leading a horse raid against an adversary—all were generally recognized as counting coup. The four feats were not only displays of courage but also the basis of a system of gaining political and social prestige.

A warrior did not distinguish himself by accumulating goods. Although his most treasured possessions probably were the weapons or horses he had captured from enemies, he often gave away these prizes to someone older or otherwise to be respected. It brought extra merit to distribute an enemy's possessions among one's kinsmen.

The value of the coup lay primarily in the tremendous skill and daring that it took to draw close enough to one's opponent to acquire the coup. For some, ermine skins worn on a shirt and wolf tails attached to moccasin heels—emblems of the number of coups achieved—were worn with pride. At any public gathering, such as a feast or dance, warriors recounted their exploits. Here, too, they distributed some of their captured possessions, demonstrating generosity.

A man could be acknowledged for his hunting or storytelling abilities, but only in counting coup was he recognized as a "good man." A man who had never gained a single coup was a "nobody." If he had at least one, he was honored. In some cultures, performing one coup of each type might make him a chief—an example of generosity, honesty, skill, and bravery.

—NEMA MAGOVERN

Kiowa drawing of a mounted warrior counting
coup on a Mexican or white man, 1875–1877.
Fort Marion, St. Augustine, Florida.

Smithsonian Institution National
Anthropological Archives. 08547604

DO INDIANS DO RAIN DANCES?

> We give thanks to all the waters of the world for quenching our thirst and providing us with strength. Water is life. We know its power in many forms—waterfalls and rain, mists and streams, rivers and oceans. With one mind, we send greetings and thanks to the spirit of water.
> —Excerpt from *Ohenton Kariwahtekwen*:
> *Greetings to the Natural World*,
> the Iroquois Thanksgiving Address

Yes, some tribes maintain the tradition of rain dances. Like all humans, Native peoples of the Americas have always understood the connection between rain and life. Traditional Native American views include a recognition that rain at the right times and in the appropriate amounts is a vital component of a well-functioning natural world. This knowledge is deep, based on the collective experiences of thousands of years. All people depend on rain to fill the rivers, to help plants grow, and to nurture life. Among groups that practice traditional agriculture, the connection to rain is even more critical. Native cultures conceptualize and participate in these relationships with the natural world in a wide range of ways. Ceremonies, prayers, ritual art, songs, and, yes, dances are among the many ways that Native people acknowledge and help to maintain the delicate balance in nature.

These spiritual and culturally important activities are not practiced randomly. They are part of complex religious cycles that occur throughout the year, year after year. Native peoples of the southwest-

ern United States nurture their crops from the time they prepare the fields through harvest. Over the centuries, Hopi people in northeastern Arizona have adapted their planting and plant breeding techniques to the arid desert climate. Most of their ceremonies are dedicated to the successful raising of crops.

> Anything that Hopis do, it's for the rain; any kind of dances, even your social dances, they still have to pray for the rain or a good summer or good days ahead. . . . It's all connected. The ceremonies are for all the people . . . throughout the world; not just for themselves; but throughout the world, for everybody . . . [to] live in harmony. . . . That's what it's all about.
>
> —Clifford Lomahaftewa (Hopi)

The importance of water is reflected in many Native cultural expressions besides dance. Among the Navajo (Diné), water symbols can be found in sandpaintings, which are created for ceremonies and destroyed upon their completion. The value of water is also evident even in Diné social structures, with clan names such as Tábąąhí (Water's Edge Clan), Tó`ahaní (Near to Water Clan), and Toʼtsóhnii (Big Water Clan) calling attention to places and lineages related to water. Across the hemisphere, water-related images are found on pottery, beadwork, carvings, weavings, and hide paintings.

In addition to supporting life, the appearance of water is also seen as a blessed cleansing of the earth. Traditional Hupa people of northern California perform an elaborate ceremony called the Jump Dance every two years to ward off disease and other disasters. At the end of the ten-day dance, they watch for rain, a sign that the Kixunai, or spirits, approve of the ceremony and that the earth is renewed.

It is hard to know when or why these important activities were first caricatured, joked about, and denigrated in American society and media. Inaccurate and stereotypical images often misrepresent Native cultures. The reality of cultural practices such as rain dances is, of course, much more meaningful and humanly rich than the popular images portray.

—EDWIN SCHUPMAN

ARE DREAM CATCHERS AN AUTHENTIC TRADITION?

Yes. Dream catchers are an authentic tradition for the Ojibwe people of the Great Lakes region. Frances Densmore (1867–1957), an ethnomusicologist who did exhaustive fieldwork among the Ojibwe (sometimes known as Chippewa or Anishinaabe), describes dream catchers as one of three types of objects that families hung from a baby's cradleboard. Each had a specific purpose: as a protective charm, as a toy, or as a diversion to keep a baby occupied. Dream catchers fell into the first category.

In her book *Chippewa Customs* (1929), Densmore wrote,

> Two articles representing spider webs were usually hung on the hoop of a child's board, and it was said that "they catch everything evil as a spider's web catches and holds everything that comes in contact with it." These articles consist of wooden hoops about three-and-a-half inches in diameter, filled with an imitation of a spider's web. In old times, the web was made of nettle-stalk twine and colored dark red with the juice of bloodroot and the inner bark of the wild plum.

In *Chippewa Child Life and Its Cultural Background*, originally published by the Smithsonian Institution's Bureau of American Ethnology in 1951, anthropologist Sister M. Inez Hilger (1891–1977) also describes similar objects hanging from baby cradleboards among the Ojibwe of Nett Lake and Vermilion, Minnesota—lands that are part of the present-day Bois Forte Reservation.

Ojibwe doll in a toy cradleboard with a dream catcher attached. Velvet panels are decorated with Ojibwe floral beadwork, early 20th c.

12/2180

Because of the dream catcher's popularity today, it can be found throughout Indian Country and beyond, as people from many different tribes make them. It seems that everyone—especially children—appreciates the legend of the dream catcher. Who among us likes to be bothered by bad dreams? Dream catchers capture the bad dreams and prevent them from entering the person being protected. Only good dreams are allowed to go through the dream catcher's web.

Traditional dream catchers were not made to last a long time. Thus, they represented the fleeting nature of childhood. Traditional Ojibwe dream catchers (which are still found today) were made with a piece of wood worked into a small circle—though the dream-catcher frame is often an irregular teardrop shape, rather than completely round. Today, however, dream catchers are made of different materials—for example, a circular metal frame can be wrapped with colored leather or suede and decorated with a variety of objects, such as colored beads and feathers.

—LIZ HILL

WHY ARE MOST INDIAN CEREMONIES AND DANCES OFF-LIMITS TO NON-NATIVE AUDIENCES?

Ceremonies, which often include dances and music, abound in Native communities across the Western Hemisphere. These ceremonies are personal and communal, private and public. They are the deepest expressions of Native American religious and spiritual beliefs. They help heal people—spiritually, emotionally, physically, and mentally. They seek to establish and maintain order in the universe. They are offered to ensure the well-being of the earth and provide for the favorable outcome of human endeavors, such as hunting, building and dedicating a new home, or planting crops. Ceremonies are solemn and important events, and, as such, they are generally not intended for observers or an audience. Practitioners, beneficiaries, and those who participate according to cultural protocols are allowed to attend. According to many Native American traditions, the presence of casual observers, no matter how respectful their intentions, could negatively affect the outcome of the event, and could conceivably do harm to the observer as well.

Many Native American cultural events, however, are shared with the public. At such events, it is acceptable to observe and occasionally participate. Sometimes, even portions of ceremonies are opened for public attendance. On these occasions, visitors are welcomed, and, often, someone from the community explains the activities for guests.

Powwows are a type of Native American social event that observers are encouraged to attend. Powwows occur in many parts of North America. They are not shows or performances, but rather intertribal cultural events that feature dances, music, and other activities. Some of the individual powwow dances are only for participants who dress in the correct regalia and know the dances. Other dances,

however, such as "intertribals," are open to anyone in the audience who wants to join in. They are dances of welcoming and fellowship, and it is appropriate to participate.

Native American communities set their own rules and regulations about opening their events to the public. If one wishes to attend a ceremony or other event, it is important to find out in advance if outside observers are acceptable. Many tribes and organizations now provide publications, websites, and other sources of information about which events are open. "When in doubt, ask" is a good axiom to keep in mind when visiting Indian Country. It is important to observe the protocols, such as asking before taking pictures, sitting or standing in the right places, and learning what portions of the event may or may not be open for public participation. It is also important to remember that American Indian reservations are tribal lands, and the laws of those communities must be obeyed. Visiting a Native American community to observe a ceremony or dance can be a profoundly enriching activity, but it must be done with measured respect for the community's values and beliefs.

—EDWIN SCHUPMAN

WHAT IS THE NATIVE AMERICAN RELIGION?

No one Native American religion exists or ever did, although many Native cultures are imbued with common spiritual principles. Each tribe has its own beliefs, cosmology, creation stories, songs, ceremonies, and worship practices for keeping balance between the physical and spirit worlds. For Native people, religion traditionally has been deeply integrated into daily life. Ceremonies and prayers complement activities such as harvesting corn, collecting medicines, hunting game, and waging war. Certain animals—Raven or Bear, among others—represent different aspects of the spiritual world. The phases of an individual's life—birth, naming, coming of age, marriage, and death—may be honored in ceremonies unique to each culture. From baby-naming ceremonies to puberty rites to clan, band, and nation ceremonies such as the Lakota Sun Dance, Native spiritual practices remain vibrant today.

Europeans brought to the Americas a heavy dose of Christian missionary fervor. In the North American colonies, Christian Indian "praying towns," established in 1646 by John Eliot, began the process of forcing Native people to give up their cultures. Even if a Native community did not fully accept Christianity, the newcomers' religion influenced traditional practices. For example, before European contact, the Chickasaws called their supreme being Ababinli, which can be translated as "sitting-above" or "dwelling-above." After Contact, this being was sometimes called Abainki, or "father-above."

Today, many Native people combine traditional practices with Christianity, many are members of various Christian denominations, and an estimated 250,000 people in the United States and Canada are members of the Native American Church. The Native American

Church has ancient roots among the Huichol people of Mexico and the tribes of the Rio Grande Valley. In the late 1800s some of these tribes were removed to Oklahoma, where they shared their religious beliefs and practices with other tribes. Formally established in 1918, the Native American Church advocates brotherhood, love, family values, self-reliance, and abstinence from alcohol. Central to the church's ceremonies is peyote (part of a small, spineless cactus called mescal), which is used as a sacrament, analogous to the bread and wine that are used as sacraments in the Catholic Church. Peyote, which may only be used by members of the Native American Church, is said to be a powerful, spiritual plant, a telescope through which one can experience God as well as the powers of fire, cedar, and other elements of creation.

Until at least the 1920s the United States government officially discouraged many traditional Native religious practices—such as pipe ceremonials, sweatlodges, vision quests, and Sun Dances. In 1883 Secretary of the Interior Henry M. Teller established Courts of Indian Offenses on reservations, which investigated, convicted, and punished Native people who followed tribal religions. It was not until 1994, after Congress had passed the American Indian Religious Freedom Act and its amendments, that Native Americans could feel protected enough to fully exercise the freedom of religion guaranteed to all citizens by the U.S. Constitution.

—MARY AHENAKEW

How can I find a shaman (or medicine man) who will teach me?

It is unlikely that you will. The knowledge possessed by medicine people is privileged, and it often remains in particular families. One is initiated into medicine knowledge as one grows older or is initiated into a particular society that "owns" specific ceremonial wisdom, rites, and accoutrements. In some tribes medicine knowledge is considered a spiritual gift, but a disciplined apprenticeship of many years is also necessary. According to the late Mathew King, a Lakota spiritual leader, "The forbidden things . . . must be learned, and the learning is very difficult. . . . For someone who has not learned how our balance is maintained to pretend to be a medicine man is very, very dangerous."

Originally condemned as heathenish by European invaders and missionaries, Native religious beliefs and traditions have been usurped since the 1970s by a number of people claiming to have insight into the deepest recesses of Native spiritual wisdom. These pseudo-shamans prey upon susceptible people who are in search of either a quick spiritual fix or something more fulfilling than their own belief systems have provided. The embezzlement of Native spirituality has been a long-standing problem that jeopardizes the survival of Native cultures. For example, the authority of traditional spiritual leaders is diminished when information provided by impostors passes for "Indian" because it fits widely held stereotypes.

Knowledgeable elders may sometimes be willing to school someone outside their tribe in the spiritual ways of their people. Non-Natives may even be allowed to participate in certain ceremonies. Sun Dances and sweatlodge ceremonies are held by various tribes all over the country. Non-Natives or members of other tribes may be invited

to join them, as long as the guests have been properly introduced and behave with respect. Certain ceremonies in the Southwest are open for public viewing but not for participation. Others, such as the Hopi Snake Dance, have been closed to outsiders for many years because of aggressive attempts to profit from the sacred ceremony. An inquiry to a Native person about religious beliefs or ceremonies is often viewed with suspicion. It is better to wait until he or she volunteers the information. If you insist on asking, be polite and respectful, and do not take offense if the answer is no.

—ARWEN NUTTALL

Do INDIANS HAVE FUNERALS?

Today, with the influence of many religions, individual beliefs differ from person to person, but all tribes traditionally had some form of afterlife as part of their belief system. In the traditional Native view, death was not an end, but rather a transition. It was an inevitable turning point at which a person emerged into a new plane of being. Beliefs about what happened when a person left this world and traveled to the next differed across tribes, as did the ritual practices and ceremonies that accompanied the newly deceased.

For most Native communities, certain codes of conduct were in place for handling the deceased and preparing the body for the soul's journey into the next world. For Zuni people, it included dressing the body in certain clothes or covering it with cornmeal. At San Juan Pueblo, relatives placed cornmeal under the arm of the deceased as sustenance for the journey. Some believed that only certain people or members of a particular group or society could handle the body. Some tribes, such as the Lakota, prescribed a specific period of mourning and the cutting of mourners' hair. For the Haudenosaunee (Iroquois), the ceremonies surrounding interment might have included feasting and gaming. Other communities practiced weeping, which ranged from silent crying to agonized wailing. Some Amazonian tribes created a drink from plantain juice and the ashes of the deceased, consuming it as a way of keeping their loved ones near them. While many may find this rite disturbing, there are cultures who think placing loved ones underground is equally unsettling. Certain rules also had to be followed so that the spirit of the dead would journey in peace. The Navajo destroyed or gave away all the belongings of the deceased. Other tribes avoided speaking the dead person's name. Placement of the body

also differed among tribes. Some buried their dead, while others cremated the bodies. Several Plains tribes placed the dead on scaffolds above the ground, or in trees.

The influence of Christianity has had a profound effect on the traditional beliefs of Native people. Many were converted to Catholicism and other Christian religions. Today most Native people bury their loved ones in coffins in cemeteries or have them cremated. Many still engage, however, in certain traditional funeral rites. Specific prayers may be recited, certain articles placed on or with the body, or rules of mourning maintained. A special group or society may prepare the body or lead specific rituals associated with encouraging the spirit along its journey. While funeral rites among Native people are diverse, they are all accompanied by deep respect and wishes to their loved one for a safe journey into the next world, whatever form it may take.

—ARWEN NUTTALL

SOVEREIGNTY

WHAT ARE THE INDIAN POPULATIONS OF THE UNITED STATES, CANADA, AND LATIN AMERICA?

According to the U.S. Census of 2000, the American Indian and Alaska Native population totals 2,475,956, or nine-tenths of 1 percent of the total population of the country. But in 2000, for the first time, people were given the chance to describe themselves as being of more than one race, and 1,643,345 people reported themselves as American Indian or Alaska Native in combination with other races. The total proportion of the population, then, who identified itself as entirely or partially American Indian was 1.5 percent. The ten states with the largest American Indian populations were (in order) California, Oklahoma, Arizona, Texas, New Mexico, New York, Washington, North Carolina, Michigan, and Alaska.

Census figures, however, should not be taken at face value, since they do not reflect those who were not counted or did not want to identify themselves as Native American. Some American Indians are suspicious of government representatives. In the past, some reservation communities did not allow census workers to complete their surveys, and independent researchers have concluded that Native Americans were undercounted in 1960 and 1970.

The indigenous population of Canada, which is growing at twice the rate of the Canadian population overall, accounts for about 3 percent of all Canadians—nearly a million people. Because Native peoples in Mesoamerica and South America don't have the same kinds of relationships with their governments that tribes in the United States have, population statistics about indigenous groups can be calculated only approximately. The best estimates suggest that about 50 million people (about 10 percent of the total population) in Latin America identify themselves as indigenous.

—GEORGETTA STONEFISH RYAN

HOW MANY INDIAN TRIBES ARE OFFICIALLY RECOGNIZED IN THE UNITED STATES TODAY? WHY IS RECOGNITION IMPORTANT?

In 2006 federally recognized American Indian tribes numbered 561. That total includes 336 tribes in the lower forty-eight states and 225 Alaska Native village corporations (since 1971, older Alaska Natives have had the option to invest in regional and village corporations rather than to live on reservations set aside for them by the federal government). Numerous other tribes, including several in Virginia and the Lumbee Tribe in North Carolina, which has more than fifty thousand members, remain unrecognized. These particular tribes, together with others—a great number of them located on the East Coast of the United States—have been granted state recognition, meaning that the states in which they are located acknowledge prior state government treaties or other state dealings with them. Many tribes, such as the Lumbee, have been awaiting federal recognition for decades.

Federal recognition—or *acknowledgment*—means that the federal government recognizes a tribe as having certain rights and powers of self-government as well as rights to services that have been granted as a result of the tribe's special relationship to the United States. This relationship goes back to the Indian Commerce Clause and the Treaty Clause of the U.S. Constitution. Today federal acknowledgment is a complex process overseen by the U.S. Bureau of Indian Affairs. Acknowledgment is determined by seven primary factors: proof that (1) the petitioner (or tribe) for federal acknowledgment has existed historically as American Indian; (2) the group (or tribe) has existed throughout history as an entity with a governing body; (3) the group shows evidence that it has governed its members (i.e., demonstrates political influence); (4) the group has a governing document and a statement of membership criteria; (5) the tribal members are

descended from a historical Indian tribe; (6) tribal members are members of that specific tribe and not of any other tribe; and (7) neither the group (or tribe) nor its members are the subject of laws that have expressly terminated or forbidden the federal relationship. Federal recognition can also be obtained through acts of Congress and federal court decisions.

Federal recognition also is important because with it, tribes are entitled to a great number of services that the federal government provides by virtue of the long-standing federal trust responsibility toward tribal governments. The services include health care, education, housing, economic development assistance, and others.

In 2005 Native Hawaiian people continued to seek federal recognition, which would grant them the same legal status as American Indian tribes, which have the right of self-government. Efforts to federally recognize Native Hawaiians have been ongoing in Congress since 1999, largely through Hawai'i's two senators, Daniel K. Inouye and Daniel Akaka (the latter of whom is Native Hawaiian).

Today, Indian gaming has also affected the way in which the general public perceives federal recognition of tribes. Under the Indian Gaming Regulatory Act (IGRA) of 1988, only federally recognized tribes in states that already allow a particular class of gambling can operate a gaming facility. Public opposition toward tribes seeking federal acknowledgment—whether or not the tribe intends to conduct gaming on its land—has been steadily growing since the mid-1990s and has even prevented some tribes from becoming federally recognized. The Eastern Pequots in Connecticut and the Schaghticoke Tribe in Rhode Island are recent examples of tribes that have had their federal acknowledgment efforts delayed or thwarted by strong public and political opposition.

—LIZ HILL

CAN INDIANS LEAVE THE RESERVATIONS? WHY DO RESERVATIONS STILL EXIST?

Indian people, as citizens of the United States, are entitled to live wherever they choose, just like other American citizens. In fact, in 2005 approximately two-thirds of Indian people in the United States lived away from reservation lands in rural areas, towns, and cities. In Canada about 58 percent of government-recognized Indians were living on reserves (the Canadian term for *reservation*), according to the census for 2000.

Reservations and reserves are made up of lands that were set aside by and for tribes when they gave up enormous portions of their original landholdings in treaties with federal governments. In the past, U.S. reservations also were created through presidential executive orders and acts of Congress, or a combination of both.

Today much original Indian reservation land in the United States is inhabited by both Indians and non-Indians. Such "checkerboarding," or splintering of lands that comprise Indian reservations, is a result of unwise federal policies, in particular, the General Allotment Act (also known as the Dawes Act) of 1887. This law mandated the conversion of Indian lands that tribes had previously held in common into smaller parcels open to individual Indian ownership. More than 90 million acres were subsequently taken from U.S. tribes as a result of the General Allotment Act. These lands fell into the hands of non-Indian landowners who could afford to purchase the parcels that Indian people lost through bankruptcies or the inability to pay newly levied taxes.

Many of the nearly 300 U.S. reservations and approximately 2,670 Canadian reserves (in Canada, many First Nations communities have rights to more than one reserve within a province or

Sign outside tribal government buildings,
Pawhuska, Oklahoma. June 2006.

Photo by Katherine Fogden (Mohawk).

territory) are incapable of sustaining agriculture and other economic
pursuits. But over the years many Indian people have come to consider the reservations "home," despite having been initially forced to
move there. Beginning in the early decades of the 1800s, for example, the government forced a number of East Coast tribes from their
ancestral homelands to faraway, inhospitable lands west of the Mississippi.

In Mesoamerica and South America, very few of the approximately 50 million indigenous people live on land set aside for them.
Some village communities in the Mesoamerican highlands and Andes
Mountains are officially recognized as the collective owners of their
lands, and some Latin American governments created reservations for
lowland peoples in the early 1900s. But most of Latin America's indigenous people live in the countryside or large cities.

Many reservations, reserves, and indigenous villages continue to
be socially and economically depressed, with very high levels of poverty and unemployment among residents, few economic opportunities, and high incidences of alcohol and drug abuse. But Indian people
who are living elsewhere often return to them to visit their families
and participate in a variety of cultural activities. Most elders were

born on the reservations or in villages, and many still live there. Reservation lands, which may or may not have been part of ancestral homelands, continue to be imbued with cultural and religious significance for the people.

—LIZ HILL

CAN INDIANS LEAVE THE RESERVATIONS? WHY DO RESERVATIONS STILL EXIST?

125

ARE ANY INDIANS LEFT ON THE EAST COAST?

Many Native peoples are located on the East Coast of the United States as well as in every other part of North, Central, and South America. But they are not the "Indians" of popular literature, commercial advertising, and Hollywood films: people with long black hair who ride horses, live in tipis, and speak in stoic grunts. Except for some indigenous people in remote parts of the Amazon who, even today, have had little or no contact with the outside world, Native Americans, including those on the East Coast, are contemporary people living contemporary lives.

Countering the prevailing wisdom that continues to place "real" Native people west of the Mississippi, many tribes still live on their traditional lands along the East Coast of the United States. They have always been there and show no signs of disappearing. A few of these communities include the Tunica-Biloxi (Louisiana); the Catawba (South Carolina); the Lumbee (North Carolina); the Mi'kmaq (Maine); the Mohegan (Connecticut); the Passamaquoddy (Vermont); the Penobscot (Maine and Canada); the Chickahominy (Virginia), the Haudenosaunee (the Onondaga, Mohawk, Seneca, Tuscarora, Cayuga, and Oneida in upstate New York and Canada), also known as the Iroquois Confederacy; the Seminole (Florida); and Miccosukee (Florida). Whether federally or state recognized, the tribes of the East Coast have governments, cultures, and traditions that have endured for centuries.

Why, then, does the stereotype remain so potent? One reason is that the Native populations of the East Coast were exposed to Europeans long before many of the indigenous peoples living west of the Mississippi. So, the eastern tribes experienced about 350 more years of assimilation than did those in the West. Intermarriage between Euro-

Marvin Bradby, chief of the Eastern Chickahominy tribe at the Six Nations Powwow, which was held in support of the six Virginia tribes seeking federal recognition, May 3, 2003. Charles City County, Virginia.

Photo by Katherine Fogden (Mohawk).

peans, African slaves, and Indian people also occurred much earlier on the East Coast. It is also true that many eastern tribes were completely extinguished by the Europeans in the early years following Contact, largely by disease and warfare.

Another reason for believing that Native peoples are no longer living on the East Coast is that beginning in 1830 with the passage of the Indian Removal Act, many eastern tribes, including the Cherokee, Chickasaw, Choctaw, Seminole, and Creek, were forcibly "removed" from their traditional East Coast homelands to territories west of the Mississippi. Small pockets of people, however, including ancestors of today's Seminole and Eastern Band of Cherokee, hid from the federal authorities and stayed behind. But most were moved west. Thousands of Native people died during the series of forced marches in 1838–1839 that became known as the Trail of Tears.

The populations of some East Coast tribes once dwindled to the point of near-extinction, but many have rebounded and are thriving. Perhaps one of the most inspirational stories concerns that of the Mashantucket Pequot people of Connecticut, who experienced near-annihilation in 1637 and whose remaining small populations were scattered in many different places. Today the tribe—which owns Foxwoods, the largest gambling enterprise in the world—is economically healthy, its culture revitalized.

—LIZ HILL

Why do American Indians run casinos?

Indian casinos are not owned by individuals, nor are they the same type of commercial gambling enterprises as those located in Las Vegas and Atlantic City. Instead, they are owned and operated by tribal governments. In the 1980s tribal governments argued that their sovereignty guaranteed them the right to open gaming enterprises to the public. A compromise with the federal government eventually resulted in the Indian Gaming Regulatory Act (IGRA). Passed by Congress in 1988, IGRA guaranteed tribes the right to conduct gaming on their reservation lands as a means of developing their economies.

Another difference between commercial casino operations and Indian gaming casinos is that the profits of the latter—by law—must support the following: Indian community infrastructure; diverse, self-sufficient tribal economies; and charitable causes. Although some tribes pay their members a share of casino revenues (called "per capita payments," or "per caps"), most do not have enough left over—after setting aside operating expenses and revenues earmarked for community needs.

Almost all states allow some form of gambling. In 2005, according to the American Gaming Association, forty-seven states and the District of Columbia allowed charitable gaming, and forty states and the District of Columbia had state lotteries. Indian gaming facilities are currently located in twenty-eight states. Perhaps the most important fact to remember is that Indian tribes are not commercial businesses or "special interest groups"; they are governments, each with its own structure, priorities, and jurisdiction. Because Indian gaming is a form of gambling that exists to provide revenue for Native tribes—much the same as state lotteries provide revenues for education and

other state needs—and because tribes are sovereign governments, government gaming is allowed on reservation lands, which are free of state jurisdiction.

The Indian Gaming Regulatory Act did not create Indian gaming; gaming had existed for a decade or more on reservations in the form of large-scale bingo games and, even earlier, in traditional games. In 1987 the Supreme Court upheld in *California v. Cabazon* the right of American Indian tribes as sovereign nations to conduct gaming on Indian lands free of state control when similar gaming is permitted by the state outside the reservation. At the same time, the IGRA affirmed that tribes had the power to conduct gaming on Indian lands but also gave states the ability to negotiate—via tribe-state compacts—gaming regulations and the kinds of games played.

—LIZ HILL

WHAT HAPPENS TO THE REVENUE FROM INDIAN CASINOS?

In accordance with the Indian Gaming Regulatory Act (IGRA), which was enacted by the U.S. Congress in 1988 to provide a new means of economic development for American Indian tribes, revenues from Indian casinos are used primarily to help rebuild Native communities. Many Native American communities in the United States remained in various stages of poverty due to neglect by the federal government, and Indian gaming was seen as a way to enable tribes to become more self-sustaining.

In 2004 a substantial portion of the estimated $18.5 billion national Indian casino revenue was used to operate, maintain, and regulate tribal gaming facilities. American Indian tribal governments used the rest of the revenues in their communities to continue building much-needed infrastructure such as police and fire stations, hospitals and health clinics, schools, day-care and Head Start facilities, elder-care centers, and sewer and water systems. Examples of facilities built with gaming revenues during the past few years include an elder citizen care center at the Mille Lacs Indian Reservation in north-central Minnesota; a hospital at the Pueblo of Isleta in New Mexico; a Head Start center for the Mandan, Hidatsa, and Arikara Nation in North Dakota; and a high school for the Mescalero Apache tribe in New Mexico—where tribal history and culture are important parts of the curriculum.

In 2004 the National Indian Gaming Association (NIGA) reported that "Indian tribes spend tribal government casino revenue as follows: 20 percent of net revenue is used for education, child and elder care, cultural preservation, charitable donations and other purposes; 19 percent goes to economic development; 17 percent to health

Tsali Manor, a Cherokee senior citizen's center
financed by revenue from the local casino.
Cherokee, North Carolina, 2003.

Photo by R. A. Whiteside.

care; 17 percent to police and fire protection; 16 percent to infrastructure; and 11 percent to housing."

Revenues from gaming casinos also give Native tribes the capital
to invest in other businesses besides gaming. A number of tribes, including the Shakopee Mdewakanton Sioux (Dakota) Community in
Minnesota, the Winnebago Tribe of Nebraska, and the Tulalip Tribes
in Washington State, have invested in convention centers, movie the-
aters, gas stations, hotels, spas and health clubs, and golf courses, thus
diversifying their economies. By doing so, communities hope that future tribal governments will be less reliant upon gaming, which many
Indian people believe will not always be the only viable means of
improving tribal economies.

Indian gaming facilities also provide revenue to federal, state,
and local communities. Through the more than 553,000 jobs that
tribal gaming generated in 2004, the federal government benefited
by receiving $5.5 billion in tax revenue and $1.4 billion in revenue

savings through reduced welfare and unemployment benefit payments. In 2004 Indian gaming also generated $1.8 billion in state revenue and $100 million more for local governments.

—LIZ HILL

Do the Rich Casino Tribes Help Out the Poor Tribes?

Yes. The more successful casino tribes do assist less-fortunate gaming and nongaming tribes. Sometimes the less-successful tribes have gaming facilities of their own that don't reap the same kinds of revenues; sometimes they do not. Unfortunately, stories about how the wealthier tribes are helping those with less robust economies do not interest the mainstream news media, and many instances of tribe-to-tribe giving also go unnoticed.

An Analysis of the Economic Impact of Indian Gaming in 2004, an annual report issued by the National Indian Gaming Association (NIGA), which represents 184 of the country's 228 gaming tribes, reported some recent examples of tribe-to-tribe generosity:

- In Arizona, Gaming Device Operating Rights have enabled tribes—including many that do not have casinos—to lease their gaming devices to other tribes in the state. In this manner, tribes that do not have casinos can generate revenues to operate their tribal governments and programs.

- The Forest County Potawatomi Tribe in Wisconsin periodically provides assistance through their gaming revenues to the Red Cliff and Mole Lake bands of Chippewa, also located in Wisconsin.

- The Shakopee Mdewakanton Sioux Community in Prior Lake, Minnesota, has an impressive tradition of charitable giving to less-fortunate tribes. In 2004 the tribe gave $1.2 million to the Yankton Sioux Tribe in South Dakota. Of that amount, $1 million

went toward developing the Yankton Sioux Tribe's Fort Randall Casino, and $150,000 went toward the tribe's Low Income Heating Energy Assistance Program, which provides emergency payments for families in need during the reservation's harsh winter months. The Shakopee Tribe also gave $1.2 million to the Mandan, Hidatsa, and Arikara Nation at Fort Berthold, North Dakota, for reservation housing projects, and they gave a $2 million development grant to the Ponca Tribe of Nebraska.

Throughout history, Indian people have been known for sharing with others. That spirit of giving continues. According to NIGA, gaming tribes are committed to providing charitable assistance to both Natives and non-Natives. In 2004 tribes donated more than $100 million to other tribes and to non-Native community and nonprofit organizations. In-kind donations—such as the thousands of Thanksgiving turkeys that the Morongo Band of Mission Indians in California has given to local and Native communities—have been a tradition for several years. That tribe and other California tribes regularly contribute to the Special Olympics, the American Cancer Society, and the Juvenile Diabetes Foundation. Many successful gaming tribes provided assistance during wildfires in Southern California in 2003, which destroyed homes on a number of reservations, and in the aftermath of Hurricane Katrina in 2005, which devastated many tribes in the South.

—LIZ HILL

WHY IS THERE STILL POVERTY ON SOME RESERVATIONS?

In August 2005 the U.S. Census Bureau reported that on a three-year average, 24.3 percent of American Indians and Alaska Natives continue to live in poverty—annual incomes remaining below about $19,350 per year for a family of four. This figure is more than twice the rate of poverty among white Americans. Based on the same three-year average, poverty in Indian Country also continues to be on the rise.

While gaming has brought a measure of financial well-being to some tribes, it has not provided enough to overcome the effects of more than a century of neglect by the federal government. Gaming has worked well for those tribes with reservations and casinos close to large urban centers. The casinos provide jobs and economic opportunity to tribal citizens as well as to many non-Natives. But for small, remote communities, economic gains have been modest, to say the least.

A wide range of social ills continues to plague reservation peoples. In addition to the age-old problems of disease, poor nutrition, and alcohol abuse, illegal drug and gang activity has devastated many Native communities. Suicide is too common, with young boys most at risk. Domestic abuse also is a problem on many reservations.

Years of neglect by, and dependence on, the federal government continue to shape the legacy that Indians on reservations have inherited. The long-standing effects of this history constitute the major reason that poverty and lack of education, among many other social and economic ills, continue to affect Indian people living on reservations. Everyday domestic comforts that average Americans take for granted—such as running water, sewer systems, housing, electricity,

heat, food, transportation, and telephone service—are often in woefully short supply on reservations. In many places, individuals hold little hope for a better life. The most immediate effect of reservation poverty is the overall lack of economic opportunity for tribal citizens. Without jobs or financial stability on their reservations, many Indians move away.

The monies made available to tribes from the federal government have accomplished only the bare minimum. Today there is a profound shift away from the idea that U.S. government support can alone solve tribal economic problems. The emphasis is on what the tribes themselves can do. A new sense of self-determination is influencing the way in which tribes operate their governments and businesses.

Since 1987 the Harvard Project on American Indian Economic Development at Harvard University has been studying social and economic development on Indian reservations and in Alaska Native villages. The project poses the question "How, amidst well-documented and widespread poverty and social distress, are an increasing number of tribes breaking old patterns and putting together economies, social institutions, and political systems that work?"

Through more than three hundred field research reports, the Harvard Project has been able to observe the systems that work and those that do not work on reservations. It is clear that dependence on the federal government has not worked. In the words of the Harvard study, "sovereignty matters." In addition, "institutions matter"—stable tribal institutions and the separation of tribal politics from business ventures. Finally, "culture matters," which is to say that "successful tribal economies stand on the shoulders of culturally appropriate institutions of self-government that enjoy legitimacy among tribal citizens."

—LIZ HILL

WHAT BENEFITS DO INDIANS RECEIVE FROM THE U.S. GOVERNMENT?

B efore the government of the United States was formed, Native American tribal peoples governed themselves, held lands in common for their members, and clearly related to one another as sovereign entities. Beginning in the earliest days of the English colonies, government-to-government treaties, court decisions, acts of Congress, and presidential actions recorded nearly two hundred years of huge American Indian contributions to state and federal landholdings. In return, tribes were offered payments, ever-smaller reservation lands, and a number of government services. Over the decades, the services have varied widely in quantity and quality. Today federally recognized tribes have access to more than six hundred government programs, including health care through the Indian Health Service (which has clinics and hospitals on a number of reservations), education grants and programs, and housing assistance.

Tribal members may be eligible for monetary payments from the federal government if, for example, the tribe has settled a land claim with the federal government and a payment is divided among individual tribal members. In some cases, the federal government leases out tribal lands for cattle grazing or other purposes. The Bureau of Indian Affairs then places the monies collected in federal trust accounts, either for individuals or the tribal government, depending upon who, specifically, owns the land. Tribal members also can exercise, often after a struggle against competing interests, the hunting and fishing rights accorded them by federal treaties.

Tribal members are eligible to apply for "Indian preference" that certain federal agencies, such as the Indian Health Service and the Bureau of Indian Affairs, have established for various federal government

In the Treaty of Traverse des Sioux, signed on July 23, 1851, the Wahpeton and Sisseton bands of the Upper Sioux ceded millions of acres of their lands in southern and western Minnesota Territory. In exchange, the U.S. government promised $1,665,000 in cash and annuities, most of which was lost or effectively stolen before it could be paid.

Meeting of Sioux leaders and U.S. government officials, Camp Traverse des Sioux, Minnesota, July 16, 1851.

Hulton Archive, © Getty Images.

jobs. Artists who are members of federally recognized tribes are also allowed by law—the 1990 Indian Arts and Crafts Act— to identify themselves as Indian artists and to advertise their products as Indian made.

Native people also receive assistance from their tribal governments. Today, owing to the success of gaming and other enterprises, members of some tribes are eligible for new and enhanced programs and services. Some—but by no means all—federally recognized tribes that engage in gaming give each of their tribal members an individual payment. College scholarships for academically eligible members, new preschool programs, and senior citizen centers are just a few of the benefits that business development has brought to entire communities.

—LIZ HILL

Do Indians Have to Pay Taxes?

Yes, Indians have to pay federal income taxes, the same as all other American citizens. In the Supreme Court case *Squire v. Capoeman* of 1956, the court stated, "We agree with the Government that Indians are citizens and that in ordinary affairs of life, not governed by treaty or remedial legislation, they are subject to the payment of income taxes as are all other citizens."

Taxation issues regarding Indian tribes have continued to be re-examined in recent years, causing much contention among the federal government, states, and tribes. Because of the ongoing debates, the general public has often been misled into thinking that Indian *individuals*, rather than *tribes*, do not pay taxes.

The difference—and confusion—often lies in the status of Indian tribes, which are governments. As such, tribes are not subject to taxation by other state or federal governments, including those of the United States. To cite a misunderstanding from recent years: Indian gaming revenues are considered tribal government revenues and are not taxed, since they are used to provide essential government services.

Two cases in which individual Indians are not taxed by the federal government are notable. In the first instance, no taxes are levied on federal monies that have been used to compensate individual Indians for the taking of their private land, such as treaty land, for government use. In the second instance, the income from trust land, the legal title to which is held by the United States, is not taxed.

With regard to state taxes, Indians living on reservations do not pay state income taxes on the income they earn while working on their reservations. Indians also do not pay state sales taxes for goods

or services purchased on their reservations, but those who live off the reservation do pay both kinds of state taxes. Because tribes are governments, however, they have the right to tax their members—and non-Indians—living on their reservations.

—LIZ HILL

An advertisement for Indian land that has been made available to white settlers, 1879.

DO INDIANS HAVE TO FOLLOW STATE HUNTING AND FISHING REGULATIONS?

Not necessarily. In the United States, Indian peoples have the right to hunt and fish their traditional lands—even if those lands are not within the current boundaries of a tribal reservation—to provide food and the other basic necessities of life for themselves and their families. Early in its history the U.S. government signed treaties with many tribes that included the continuance of these rights in perpetuity.

Because Indian tribes hold the right to self-government, they also have the right to regulate the hunting and fishing activities of their citizens. It is because tribes are governments that state hunting and fishing laws do not apply to Indian people who hunt and fish on their traditional lands.

With the increase of non-Indian commercial and sport hunting and fishing, however, have come inevitable conflicts. Some of the clashes have led to lengthy litigation and even violence. According to Stephen L. Pevar in his book *The Rights of Indians and Tribes: The Basic ACLU Guide to Indian and Tribal Rights* (1992), "Few areas of Indian law have created more conflict than Indian hunting, fishing, and gathering rights."

He continues:

> The right to hunt and fish was expressly guaranteed to many tribes in their treaties with the United States.
> However, this right is presumed to exist even if the treaty does not mention it. As the Supreme Court explained in 1905, a treaty is not a grant of rights to the Indians, but a taking of rights from them. Consequently, if a treaty is silent

Movie star Marlon Brando supports a Native fish–in demonstration at the Nisqually and Puyallup rivers, south of Tacoma, Washington, March 2, 1964.

© Seattle Post-Intelligencer Collection:
Museum of History and Industry/CORBIS.

on the subject of Indian hunting and fishing rights, then these rights are not limited by the treaty and still exist in full force.

In the twentieth and twenty-first centuries, state laws that regulate hunting and fishing have often clashed with Indian hunting and fishing rights, especially when Indian people's traditional hunting and fishing grounds are off their reservation lands. In recent decades several notable cases have challenged Indian rights to subsistence hunting and fishing. One well-known example concerns several Washington State tribes.

In Washington the state fishing law dictated in 1963 that all Indians needed to fish with hooks and line rather than their traditional nets. The ruling completely disregarded the treaties that had been established with the tribes in the mid-1800s. In 1964 the conflict became violent in an incident in which the police brutalized Indian people who had gathered to fish at Frank's Landing on the Puyallup River, south of Tacoma. By 1973 the federal government, which represented fourteen of the tribes, sued the state of Washington. The court decision, which became known as the Boldt Decision, came down in favor of the tribes and upheld their original treaty rights. In 1979 the Supreme Court agreed, supporting Boldt's original ruling.

—LIZ HILL

DO MUSEUMS HAVE TO GIVE BACK EVERYTHING IN THEIR COLLECTIONS THAT WAS TAKEN FROM TRIBES WITHOUT PERMISSION?

Museums and American Indian tribes have had a difficult and complicated history. Many tribes face the agonizing reality that some of their ancestors' remains, as well as the sacred objects buried with them, were taken without permission and eventually made their way into museum collections. In addition to those items taken from burial sites, countless other objects of cultural importance—some considered sacred and strictly ceremonial—were excavated, stolen, traded, and occasionally purchased outright. The eight-hundred-thousand-object collection at the Smithsonian's National Museum of the American Indian (NMAI), in fact, is the result of the obsession of German American banker George Gustav Heye (1874–1957), who sent collectors on expeditions to indigenous communities in Canada, Peru, Patagonia, Chile, Alaska, and throughout the continental United States. In 1924 alone, he amassed more than twenty-two thousand objects. Although Heye was greatly concerned about the diversity and authenticity of his collection, he cared far less about how objects were acquired.

Nearly a century after he bought the first item in his vast collection (a hide shirt), Heye's entire legacy was transferred to the newly established National Museum of the American Indian. The NMAI Act of 1989 (Public Law 101–185), which created the museum and its policies, included specific requirements for all Smithsonian museums regarding the repatriation, or return, of American Indian, Alaska Native, and Native Hawaiian human remains and objects in their collections. The new law not only allowed individual descendants, American Indian tribes, Alaska Native clans or villages, and Native Hawaiian organizations to rightfully claim their human

Cape Fox Tlingit community members, dressed in clan regalia, wait on the dock as the boat containing their repatriated Kaats totem pole pulls into the harbor, August 2001. Ketchikan, Alaska.

Photo by NMAI staff.

remains and cultural items, but it also required each museum to work proactively with tribes to inventory, identify, and return these sacred cultural objects. Heralding a new era in museum-tribal relations, Congress a year later signed another bill into law—known as NAGPRA (Native American Graves Protection and Repatriation Act)—which empowered tribes to claim their human remains and cultural items from federal collections and non-Smithsonian museums. Museum, archaeological, American Indian, historical, and religious organizations across the country immediately stepped forward to support what they considered a long-overdue mandate on behalf of Native people and communities.

Proving a direct connection to a given item, however, requires a great deal of research and documentation; the process of repatriation, therefore, is long and complex for both museums and tribes. Museums are not under orders to return all American Indian objects in their collections, but they must inventory portions of their holdings

Soaring twenty feet, and keeping a watchful eye on the visitors who pass by, is Kaats the Bear Hunter—a traditional figure in the Bear Clan of the Saxman Tlingit people of Ketchikan, Alaska. Through time, Saxman, or Cape Fox, Tlingit community members have honored the story of Kaats by carving totem poles with his image, painting them in bold colors, and placing them outside their homes. In the early 1900s one such Bear Clan totem pole was taken without permission, together with countless other cultural objects, from the Cape Fox community. The forty-foot totem pole eventually made its way to George Gustav Heye's collection in New York City and became part of the National Museum of the American Indian's collection.

The Cape Fox community never forgot about its lost Bear Clan totem, however, and they approached the museum in the late 1990s to request the return of the pole. Working closely with the community, staff at NMAI extensively researched the totem's history, and they repatriated the pole in 2001. To express gratitude for the safe return of the totem, the Cape Fox Native Corporation presented a twenty-foot cedar log to the NMAI. The museum then asked Tlingit carver Nathan Jackson and his family to use the log to create a new totem. Jackson again featured the traditional stories of Kaats. Using traditional carving techniques and colors, Jackson, his wife, Dorica, and his son Stephen created in 2004 a new totem for the NMAI, dividing the pole into three sections so that it could travel more easily from their home in Alaska to the new museum in Washington, D.C. As one of the museum's large "landmark objects," the totem pole serves as a gathering point for visitors.

For a picture of the new Kaats totem pole, see page 205.

and make those findings available to tribal representatives who request them. When a tribe can prove the ownership and cultural significance of an object, museums are required to repatriate it. Although the NMAI is active in its repatriation efforts, its collections will not be depleted, for most of its objects are not eligible for repatriation. Within the NMAI collection, approximately twenty-five thousand objects fall within the four categories of items—human remains, funerary objects, sacred objects, and objects of cultural patrimony—

identified for repatriation by the NMAI Act and its 1996 amendment, which further defined the categories.

In most cases museum and tribal representatives work very closely throughout the process. For example, tribal delegations often visit the NMAI's Cultural Resources Center in Maryland, where they can view their tribe's material collections and begin discussions with the museum's Office of Repatriation. Since 1989 the NMAI has returned approximately two thousand items to more than a hundred Native communities throughout the Western Hemisphere.

Once an object is repatriated, tribes can display it in their museums, if it is the type of item that can or should be kept in a public collection. Some items should not be viewed publicly at all, or handled by anyone other than religious leaders. Age and poor condition require special care of some items, so once they are returned to the community, fragile pieces are only moved, used, or worn during ceremonies or special occasions. When cultural and sacred items are returned by museums, it is a cause for celebration and, sometimes, solemn ceremony—honoring and welcoming the objects back to their rightful home.

—TANYA THRASHER

How Does Someone Become a Tribal Chief?

Historically each tribe was a sovereign entity with the right to determine for itself how best to choose its formal leaders. Leaders assumed their roles in a variety of ways: by birthright; through community election; through selection by members of their clans; by performing an auspicious deed or act of bravery benefiting the entire community; or through spiritual insights and an ability to guide the community spiritually. "Separation of church and state" did not exist among tribes. Religion and government were inextricably intertwined, with some leaders, such as those of the Aztec, Inka, and Maya, considered spiritually guided and worshipped by people of lower social status. In many traditional Native societies men and women could share leadership.

Leaders of tribes and other groups of indigenous Americans were known by a variety of titles. The names used to designate specific kinds of chiefs—political, religious, village, or clan, for example—varied from tribe to tribe. The Hawaiian Islands were governed by a monarchy—the leaders were kings and queens, and royalty was called *ali'i.* In the northeastern United States some tribes called their leaders *sachems.*

Today the leaders of American Indian tribes—many of whom were formerly referred to as chiefs by a mostly non-Native public—are still known by many titles, including that of chief. Some of the more common titles include chairman (chairwoman or chairperson), governor, and president. Regardless of the word used, these titles signify a person who has been selected by his or her tribal members as their top leader, a designation that, at least for the 561 tribes that have been federally recognized as sovereign nations, is equal in importance to that of the U.S. president or any other chief of state.

With the Indian Reorganization Act of 1934, lands that had been previously taken from tribes began to be restored, and tribal government reform was introduced. Most tribes adopted the recommendations of the Indian Reorganization Act and reorganized their tribal governments according to written constitutions. At issue, of course, is the origin of the constitutions in non-Native systems.

Many traditional Native forms of governance have ceased to exist altogether. Today's tribal leaders govern with the assistance of a tribal council, a governing body that is also elected by tribal members.

—LIZ HILL

ANIMALS AND LAND

What Kinds of Animals Mean the Most to Indians?

Although animals and other nonhuman life, such as plants and rocks, have historically held enormous significance for many Native peoples, no one animal can be said to carry the greatest meaning for all American Indians. Depending on the tribe, bears, eagles, wolves, buffalo, or any one of many other animals may be given familial titles such as *father*, *brother*, or *uncle*, and human traits, such as the ability to talk, sing, and reason. Animals can be endowed with supernatural powers.

For some Native peoples, certain fish, such as the Hawaiian *akule*, a type of shad, is considered to be a gift from the Creator. Native Hawaiians also believe that stones and other inanimate objects contain life forces that can alter the way in which humans live out their lives. In Alaska and Canada, beautifully carved Inuit wood, ivory, fur, and feather masks often represent animal spirits.

The importance of animals to Native cultures is evident in the creation stories of many tribes. Specific animals may vary from tribe to tribe, but they usually play an instrumental role. In the Ojibwe creation story the little muskrat finds some soil to give to the trickster Nanaboozhoo, who is floating in a vast sea created by a great flood that has killed off the first peoples of the earth. A turtle offers its back to Nanaboozhoo as a place for the soil. In the Mojave creation story Frog Woman kills the Great Spirit Matavilya. For the Miccosukee people, animals wait patiently in a large shell for earth to be formed. The animals are the first living beings to emerge into the newly created world. A duck and a turtle figure prominently in the Arapaho creation story, while the turtle, woodpecker, and hog are integral to the Taíno creation narrative.

Yup'ik mask representing Takiokook, the king salmon that drives the fish into the Kuskokwim River, ca. 1910. Napaskiak, Alaska.

Photo by R. A. Whiteside. 9/3574

For a number of tribes, animals act as heads of clans or lineages stemming from the male (patrilineal) or female (matrilineal) sides of large, extended family groups. The Oneida people in Wisconsin, for example, have four clans: wolf, bear, eagle, and turtle. Like other tribes that have animals as representatives of their clans (such as other Haudenosaunee [Iroquois] people and the Ojibwe, to name just a few), each animal—and the people that belong to its clan—is imbued with special characteristics, such as leadership (eagle), medicine keeping (bear), providing direction in life (wolf), and caring for the environment (turtle).

Hundreds of years ago many Native peoples were hunters and gatherers. Hunting was not considered a sport; rather, it was one of the most important activities in which (primarily) the men of the community engaged. In prayers or rituals, hunters expressed respect for the animal before, during, and after the kill. Animals such as the buffalo were considered gifts from the Creator, and great care was taken in preparation for the hunt. Among Alaska Native peoples today, subsistence hunting and fishing continues to be a way of life and an important part of their cultures. For the Makah, whaling, which they have done for thousands of years, is an important reaffirmation of their cultural identity.

—LIZ HILL

WHAT IS THE RELATIONSHIP OF NATIVE AMERICANS TO THE ENVIRONMENT?

In the 1970s, America's imagination was captured by the "Keep America Beautiful" television ad, which featured a purported Native American dressed in traditional regalia with a tear running down his cheek at the site of polluted land and water. While that vivid image has some basis in traditional values, it is overly simplistic.

Traditional Native American sensibilities regarding the earth and the human relationship with it are elucidated in these words of the writer, actor, and chief Luther Standing Bear from his book, *Land of the Spotted Eagle* (1978): "The Lakota was a true naturist—a lover of Nature. He loved the earth and all things from the earth. . . . From Wakan Tanka there came a great unifying life force that flowed in and through all things—the flowers of the plains, blowing winds, rocks, trees, birds, animals—and that was the same force that had been breathed into the first man. Thus all things were kindred and brought together by the same Great Mystery."

As people who see themselves as part of the natural world—not separate from it—Native Americans come from cultures that value balance and strive to live in a way that respects and preserves it. When things become imbalanced, sickness, unhappiness, and confusion are the results. Then it is the human responsibility to take steps, including conducting ceremonies, to restore the balance and harmony necessary for the appropriate functioning, not only of humans but also of all things.

Like all people, Natives have traditionally obtained food, clothing, tools, transportation, homes, and medicines from the environments in which they have lived. Because Native Americans are tied philosophically and spiritually to their resources, however, they treat

A gathering place for traders and salmon fishers for thousands of years, Celilo Falls, on the Columbia River in Oregon, was submerged by the opening of The Dalles hydroelectric dam on March 10, 1957. Today the Columbia River is broken up by nineteen hydroelectric dams, and the 14 million wild salmon that inhabited the river in 1855 have dwindled to fewer than one hundred thousand.

Native fishers spearing salmon from wooden scaffolds at Celilo Falls, ca. 1940.

Hulton Archive, © Getty Images.

them with respect. Native Americans express veneration not only in ceremonies but also in the careful management of certain resources.

Before the arrival of Europeans, many Native Americans used their knowledge of the environment in the practice of agriculture. With fire and tools they cleared trees and brush to make room for fields of corn, beans, and squashes. Companion-planting the three crops helped rejuvenate the nitrogen in the soil, keep insect infestations down, and maintain moisture in the soil. As described by Doug MacCleery on the Eco-Watch Dialogues page of the USDA Forest Service website, Native Americans across North America also cleared vast tracts of land with fire to "improve game habitat, facilitate travel, reduce insect pests, remove cover for potential enemies, enhance conditions for berries, drive game, and for other purposes."

Many modern Native Americans feel these traditional connections to the earth. Communities still practice their traditional arts, agriculture, and ceremonies related to the environment. In response to modern challenges, many tribal governments are addressing environmental issues that affect their communities. The Karuk tribe of northern California is one of many that have fought to preserve salmon spawning runs in the rivers of the Northwest. Power-generating dams built on rivers in the mid-twentieth century severely depleted salmon runs. That encroachment not only interrupted the ancient cultural connection to the salmon but also affected the diet of tribal members, such as the Karuks, who believe that epidemics of obesity, heart disease, and early-onset diabetes are related to the dams. In another example, the Colville tribal members of Washington State recently rejected an opportunity to open a molybdenum (a metal used to harden steel and dye plastics) mine on their reservation. While the mine would have offered some economic opportunities, it was rejected on the basis of its impact on the reservation environment and traditional culture.

The late Native American scholar and philosopher Vine Deloria Jr. (Standing Rock Sioux) described the difference between Western and Native American understandings of the universe in an interview published in 2000:

> I think the primary difference is that Indians experience and relate to a living universe, whereas Western people— especially scientists—reduce all things, living or not, to objects. The implications of this are immense. If you see the world around you as a collection of objects for you to manipulate and exploit, you will inevitably destroy the world while attempting to control it. Not only that, but by perceiving the world as lifeless, you rob yourself of the richness, beauty, and wisdom to be found by participating in its larger design.

—EDWIN SCHUPMAN

WHAT MEANINGS DO ROCKS AND STONES HAVE FOR NATIVE AMERICANS?

Rocks and stones have always been important to Native American cultures. Rocks have served as records of the past, providing the backdrops on which Indians have painted and carved memory aids for songs, clan affiliations, visions, dreams, and grave sites. The Catawba people of the Piedmont region, like tribes elsewhere, mined their local hills for the raw quartz that they turned into arrowheads, spear points, knives, and scrapers. They also quarried soapstone, which they shaped into bowls, cooking utensils, and ceremonial pipes. Over the centuries the versatility of stone has led to some interesting uses. The Tehuelche people of Patagonia crushed gypsum into a powder they sprinkled like modern talcum on their babies. Grinding rocks has also been a way to make the colorful pigments that people everywhere use for painting and other arts.

Aside from their practical uses in making tools and weapons, rocks play roles in Native spirituality and religion. In sweatlodges, rocks are heated and piled in the center. These rocks are referred to as Grandfather Rocks or Stone People, which are names of respect that equate the rocks to ancestors. The steam released from the Grandfather Rocks during a sweat is often regarded as the breath and guidance of previous generations. Rocks appear in other spiritual settings as well. The Taíno, who inhabited the islands where Columbus landed, believed their deities lived in rocks and trees, so they carved representations of their deities into stone. These figurines, called Zemis, were viewed as intermediaries to the supernatural world and protectors of the Taíno people. The Maya also valued stone for its ability to safeguard the spirit, and they were known to place small pieces of jade in the mouths of their dead to ensure the spirit's survival.

(Below) Because it is an accretionary lava ball, this stone, from Keamoku Lava Flow near Hilo, Hawai'i, is the youngest of the Cardinal Direction stones that mark the northern, southern, eastern, and western boundaries of the landscape surrounding the National Museum of the American Indian.

Photo by Katherine Fogden (Mohawk).

(Above) The Cardinal Direction Marker on the north side of the National Museum of the American Indian landscape. This stone, from Acasta Lake, Northwest Territories, Canada, is 3.9 billion years old and among the oldest known stones on earth.

Photo by Katherine Fogden (Mohawk).

Rocks and gems have decorated the people and places of many societies. The precious stones used in jewelry have sustained a livelihood for Native artists of the past and present, who have sold their work around the world. Such enterprise once established the prominence of the Olmec stone carvers of the Gulf of Mexico, whose wares traveled all across the Western Hemisphere from 900 BC to 400 BC, finding a place in the clothing, burials, and even shamanistic rituals of groups far away.

Different tribes put rocks to different uses, but the rocks reflected similar values. Among these common values is a connection to tribal forebears, a reverence for who and what existed in the past, and a view of the earth as a living entity.

—JENNIFER ERDRICH

Is it true that Native Americans hunted a great number of large animals to extinction?

There continues to be a debate in scientific circles about whether or not Paleo-Indian peoples living on the American continent during the thousands of years before and during the Pleistocene epoch (1.8 million to about ten thousand years ago—this was also known as the period of the ice ages) contributed to the extinction of the great variety of animals that were known to have inhabited the land. The existence of an incredible array of plant, animal, bird, and other nonhuman life in the Western Hemisphere during the ice ages is not in doubt. What is less certain is exactly how all of these living beings disappeared during a relatively short period about ten thousand years ago. Did the ancestors of today's Native peoples hunt and kill large numbers to extinction? One theory suggests that they did. Another argues, however, that climatic and environmental changes caused by retreating glaciers wiped out many North American creatures, both large and small.

Most scientists believe that it was also during the Pleistocene, approximately fifteen thousand years ago, that waters receded in the strait that linked Siberia and Alaska, thus creating a "land bridge" that made it possible for people to make their way onto the North American continent. This theory—which is vigorously debated by scientists and Native peoples, many of the latter believing their ancestors have always been on the continent—contends that successive generations of northern nomadic peoples, traveling in small bands, made their way from Alaska to southern South America. Their numbers grew along the way—some scientists believe that the population could have grown relatively quickly into the millions. Certainly, when one looks at the population estimates for the Western Hemisphere

just before Columbus's arrival, with indigenous peoples perhaps numbering more than 70 million, the idea doesn't seem farfetched.

There is no doubt that the array of animals living on the American continent was at one time significantly more diverse than it is today. In *1491: New Revelations of the Americas before Columbus* (2005), Charles C. Mann describes the scene as an "impossible bestiary of lumbering mastodon, armored rhinos, great dire wolves, saber tooth cats and ten-foot-long glyptodonts like enormous armadillos." He continues, "Beavers the size of armchairs; turtles that weighed almost as much as cars; sloths able to reach tree branches twenty feet high; huge, flightless, predatory birds like rapacious ostriches—the tally of Pleistocene monsters is long and alluring."

Then, suddenly, all of these beasts were gone, rapidly disappearing from the earth around ten thousand years ago. Today's relatively small indigenous population may make it difficult to imagine a late-Pleistocene continent teeming with humans, but one theory raises the possibility that the animals could have been killed off by human overhunting. The other argument—equally convincing—is that the end of the last ice age killed off the animals. Lending more weight to the second theory is the simultaneous disappearance of plants and other nonanimal species during that time of great climatic disruption.

Some evidence, however, supports the theory that some Native cultures, such as the Maya of Central America, may have depleted their natural resources—including animal life—thus contributing to their own eventual collapse. But more recently it was Europeans and Americans who nearly exterminated the North American buffalo, and commercial whalers—not indigenous people—who drove whales to the brink of extinction.

—LIZ HILL

DO NATIVE AMERICANS STILL RIDE HORSES?

Yes. Since the 1700s, horses have been integral to Native cultures in the western United States and Canada. During the Pueblo Revolt of 1680 the Spanish, who had dominated the Pueblo peoples for the previous one hundred years, were driven south of the Rio Grande. The departing conquistadores left behind some of their horses, which the Pueblo peoples of the Southwest traded to neighboring tribes. The horses thrived and spread rapidly north and east. In providing a way to hunt buffalo more efficiently over great distances, horses not only helped many Plains cultures to flourish but also became indispensable to Plains Indian life. Horse capturing became an art, giving away horses proved one's generosity, and horse trappings were made with exquisite care.

One of the most well-known examples of a Columbia Plateau horse culture is the Nez Perce. In the early 1800s the Lewis and Clark Expedition traveled through the Nez Perce lands. The Indians welcomed the expedition and offered the explorers supplies and shelter as they made their way down the Columbia River. Meriwether Lewis wrote about the Nez Perce horses: "Their horses appear to be of an excellence, they are lofty, elegantly formed, active, and durable, in short, many of them look like fine English coursers and would make a figure in any country."

By 1863, Euro-American settlers wanted Nez Perce land and began to move the Native people out. In 1877 the U.S. Army took the land by force. Faced with the prospect of being herded onto a smaller reservation in Idaho, the Nez Perce set out for freedom in Canada with 750 men, women, and children—and two thousand horses. After months of flight and battle, the army hunted them down and removed

the men to Fort Leavenworth, Kansas. Their varicolored, or "pied," horses, which came to be called A Palouse Horse or Appaloosas, were stolen by the soldiers. But the Nez Perce, some of whom were allowed to return to the Northwest in 1885, did not forget their horses.

In 1994 the Nez Perce tribe, with the help of others, launched a horse program in which Nez Perce youth learn tribal history along with horse care and breeding. In 1998 the community developed a new breed of horse. This new Appaloosa will keep the Nez Perce horse-breeding traditions alive for generations to come.

While capturing raids are no longer carried out, horse giveaways and beautiful trappings are still very much a part of powwows and other celebrations for Plains tribes. Horses still are the subjects of songs, stories, paintings, and dances. Native people own cattle ranches and compete in horsemanship trials and rodeos. With young riders as full participants, traditional horse care, horse events, and horse-centered ceremonies remain a big part of Indian lives in the West.

—NEMA MAGOVERN

WHY DO INDIANS WEAR FEATHERS? WHY ARE EAGLE FEATHERS SO IMPORTANT TO INDIANS?

Known as the Thunderbird in many Native American cultures, the eagle is said to be the messenger between humans and the Creator, flying higher and seeing farther than any other bird. The feathers of the eagle, which help send messages to the Creator, represent prayers. Eagle feathers are used in ceremonies, worn as part of powwow regalia, or given away as honoring gifts—all to show respect to the eagle and maintain a spiritual and physical connection to this sacred creature.

Greatly prized, eagle feathers are often handed down from one generation to the next, both individually and as part of a person's regalia. The feathers are either obtained naturally—from eagles that have died or molted—or from the National Eagle Repository in Denver, Colorado, a government facility where members of federally recognized tribes can legally acquire them. Recognizing the ceremonial value of eagles to American Indians, lawmakers granted this important exception to the Bald Eagle Protection Act of 1940 (amended in 1962 to include golden eagles), which makes it illegal for anyone to possess eagle feathers or eagle parts.

Powwow dancers consider eagle feathers to be the most important item of their dress, and any part of an eagle used by a dancer—the beak, talons, and bones, for example—are treated with respect and honor. Eagle feathers are treated with great care throughout the powwow in many ways. If an eagle feather accidentally falls off a dancer's clothing during a powwow dance, a war veteran or the Arena Director will stand next to the feather to protect it. At the end of the dance, the powwow arena is cleared and a ceremony is held to retrieve the feather. In addition, feathers are often given away to dancers formally

William H. Rau. Portrait of a Sioux man, entitled *Chief Iron Tail—Sinte Maza*, ca. 1901. North or South Dakota?

P27530

entering the arena for the first time, or to celebrate an individual achievement.

In the past, tribal warriors earned eagle feathers when they demonstrated bravery, either in battle or on the hunt. Sometimes a feather would be painted or cut in a certain way to tell the story of how the feather was earned. For many non-Native people, the image of an elder or tribal leader wearing a long eagle-feather war bonnet is powerful and familiar. Plains Indian leaders and warriors did wear these beautiful headdresses— and still do today for ceremonial purposes. Wearing eagle feathers in such a way indicates rank or personal achievement.

Today as in centuries past, Native people use feathers of all kinds to decorate their dance wear, stabilize arrow shafts, weave elaborate robes and cloaks, and adorn baskets or jewelry. Tribes in certain regions honor hawks, kingfishers, ravens, woodpeckers, and hummingbirds. For many, these unique creatures of the air have great spiritual significance; by using and wearing the feathers of these birds, one can access their powers and honor them.

—TANYA THRASHER

LANGUAGE
AND
EDUCATION

Is IT TRUE THAT INDIAN LANGUAGES ARE NOW EXTINCT?

Not all Native languages are extinct. While the exact number of languages in the Western Hemisphere before 1492 can never be known, at least 300 different languages were spoken in North America and possibly as many as 1,800 spoken in Mesoamerica and South America. Fewer than 175 languages remain in North America and, of those, only about 20 are spoken by children. The Navajo language remains the most vital, with more than one hundred thousand speakers. Other fairly robust languages include Cree, Cherokee, and Yup'ik.

Mesoamerican and South American languages have generally fared better than languages farther north, although many are extinct and others are endangered. Approximately fifty million indigenous people (about 10 percent of the population) in Latin America speak between four hundred and seven hundred Native languages. The Quechuan language family is the largest, with 8.5 million speakers. In three countries an indigenous language, together with Spanish, is the official language: Quechua in Peru, Aymara in Bolivia, and Guaraní in Paraguay. While the overall numbers of speakers of indigenous languages might seem large, the Native peoples of Latin America are nonetheless under enormous pressure to adopt the predominant national language (either Spanish or Portuguese, depending on the country) as their one and only tongue.

Government policies and pressures from the dominant society are the root causes of language loss. The goal of government policies in the late nineteenth century switched from the destruction to the assimilation of Native North American societies. Missionaries and, later, the U.S. government forcibly removed children from their families

Julianna Coté (Osage) in her Osage language
class, writing the word for the color blue.
September 2006. Skiatook, Oklahoma.

Photo by Katherine Fogden (Mohawk).

and placed them in government-run boarding schools. When they arrived at the schools, teachers and administrators cut their hair, made
them wear European clothing, and replaced their Native names with
English names. Children were punished, often severely, for speaking
their Native languages. Outside the schools, fear and ridicule compelled some Native parents to stop teaching their traditional languages
to their children, while others saw the exclusive use of English as the
only way to survive economically. The heartbreaking result was that
many who went through the boarding-school system and then returned to their communities could no longer communicate with their
own people. Well into the late twentieth century, the humiliation
many adults had faced in the boarding schools kept them from at-
tempting to relearn their lost tongues or encouraging their children
to speak them.

Until relatively recent developments in formulating written Native languages, Native speakers passed their languages to others only
through speaking and listening. A great deal of the knowledge of a
people—cultural, spiritual, medicinal, cosmological—is carried in the
language. With the loss of language comes the loss of an immense
accumulation of cultural knowledge, history, and beliefs. The U.S.

government's assimilation policy was effective in diminishing the strength of Native languages, but it did not wipe them out completely.

A strong language revitalization movement is under way today. The emphasis on language as the bearer of culture has encouraged many tribes to introduce their languages to children at earlier ages and to continue language education for older kids. Some tribes have programs whereby traditional speakers work in day-care or Head Start programs, while other communities have developed language-immersion programs and even entire language-immersion schools. Many tribes are working with linguists to create a written version of their language to preserve it. Others have taken advantage of different technologies to maintain and pass along their language. The Cherokee Nation of Oklahoma, the Blackfeet Nation, and Native Hawaiians are just a few of the tribal groups that maintain repositories of print and digital language materials.

Colonization and contemporary influences have done much to erode Native languages, but the resilience that characterizes Native societies can be found in their struggle to ensure that traditional languages are spoken for generations to come.

—ARWEN NUTTALL AND LIZ HILL

DID INDIANS HAVE ALPHABETS AND WRITING BEFORE CONTACT WITH EUROPEANS?

The answer to this question may depend on how broadly one defines "writing." The narrow definition preferred by academics describes writing as a visible record based on sound and language structure, which can be interpreted by someone outside the language. Native people did not have alphabets, the basic symbols that stand for a sound, before European contact. Some Native peoples, however, especially in Mesoamerican cultures, had pictographic forms of written communication that relayed complex narratives with subtlety and detail.

In the Maya system, words as well as full sentences could be represented. At the time of Spanish invasion the Mexica (Aztec) relied heavily on a pictographic system. Pictographs illustrate ideas, not words, but Mexica artisans depicted some words and sounds. Writing in Mesoamerican cultures, which was reserved primarily for the elite, centered on genealogies, political history, and the calendrical system.

Forms of visual communication existed in North America, but none that a non-Native academic would call "writing." Petroglyphs and pictographs carved and painted on rock surfaces, for example, could convey messages, ideas, stories, or events. Many Plains tribes used pictography on buffalo hides—called winter counts—to maintain historical records. Each year, a writer added a new image that depicted the most memorable occurrence since the previous winter. Northeastern historians sealed treaties, recorded events, or communicated messages with wampum (valuable beads made out of the shell of the quahog clam).

Native people have strong oral traditions. Histories, stories, and religious rites were passed from the memories of one generation to the next through the spoken word. The world view of Native people

Sequoyah with the Cherokee syllabary he invented. Engraving of an oil painting by Charles Bird King, 1828.

Reproduced in Thomas Loraine McKenney and James Hall's *History of the Indian Tribes of North America.* Philadelphia: 1837–1844. P27706

is intricately woven into the fabric of language and ways of speaking. The oral tradition connects past, present, and future and tightens tribal and familial bonds. Before European contact, the need for writing did not exist, except in Mesoamerica, where the populations in certain areas were much greater and the leadership was organized more hierarchically than in North America. Development of written Native languages after Contact was both a Native adaptation to the dominant society and a technique by which non-Natives tried to convert Native people to Christianity.

The first instance of a written Native language developed by a Native person in North America was the Cherokee syllabary, created in 1819 by a Cherokee man named Sequoyah. While he borrowed the concept of writing from Europeans, Sequoyah's accomplishment is all the more impressive because he could neither read nor speak English. His writing system was not an alphabet but rather a set of symbols, each of which stood for the sound made by one or two consonants and a following vowel. Within a year, thousands of Cherokee people learned to read and write with the syllabary, and Cherokee scholars translated several English texts. In 1828 the first American Indian newspaper, the *Cherokee Phoenix*, was published.

Language loss was part of the systematic destruction or assimilation of Native peoples. Some languages have vanished completely, while many others are weakened. Elders believe if the language is lost, the people will be, too. Teachers, elders, and linguists have been working to capture Native speech in written form as a way to pass on the languages—and cultures—to younger generations.

—ARWEN NUTTALL

What is a Winter Count?

Native peoples of the Great Plains, such as the Lakota and Kiowa, made winter counts. Symbolic drawings representing important tribal events, epidemics, wars, and natural phenomena were painted on animal—most often buffalo—hides. Many Plains peoples considered the beginning of winter the start of a new year, and time was calculated in snow seasons.

Elders passed down winter counts—records that documented tribal history—from generation to generation within the community. Each year, the artist who was keeper of the winter count would meet with a council of elders to decide on the event or combination of events that should represent the year. The council also decided what symbols should be used. One hide robe could have well over seventy years of historical occasions represented by as many as two hundred drawings.

The keeper, who had to have a good memory to recall the experiences represented on the robe, could recite in detail those of each year, using the pictographs as memory cues. On some winter count robes the drawings were configured in the shape of a spiral, with the earliest year drawn in the center and the succeeding years coiling outward. Others were configured with the pictograph for the first year drawn on an outer edge of the robe and the following years drawn spiraling inward toward the center.

Winter counts were exhibited to the community at certain times during the year so that the history of the tribe could be shared and the meanings of symbols could be learned and passed along to the next generation. Historians later designed winter counts with the pictographs in rows from left to right. Bull Plume, a Piikuni (or North Piegan, part of the Blackfoot Confederacy) tribal member, compiled

Winter count or calendar by Shunka Ishnala (Lone Dog, life dates unknown), ca. 1800–1870. South Dakota.

Photo by Ernest Amoroso. 1/617

Detail from the Lone Dog winter count. The three figures in the center, from left to right, depict events for 1835–1836 (Lame Deer shot a Crow Indian with an arrow, drew it out, and shot him again with the same arrow); 1834–1835 (Chief Medicine Hat was killed. The figure shows a bloody body topped with an unstained war bonnet); and 1833–1834 (the year the stars fell. This was a great meteor shower observed all over the United States on November 12, 1833. In this depiction, the moon is black and the stars red).

from five original hides one of the longest winter counts in existence— not on an animal hide but in a notebook. His winter count recorded major events for each year from 1764 to 1917.

—MARY AHENAKEW

Why Was the Navajo Language Chosen for Military Code in World War II? Were All Indian "Code Talkers" Navajo?

In 1942, as the United States was entering World War II, Philip Johnston, a non-Native veteran of World War I raised on the Navajo Reservation, suggested that the Marine Corps use the Navajo language as a code. Like most Indian languages, the Navajo language was so intricate and difficult to learn that few people outside the tribe could speak it—and it was a resource unique to the United States. Moreover, with a population of nearly fifty thousand at that time, the Navajo offered a large pool of Native American recruits who spoke their language fluently. Using four Navajo volunteers, Johnston gave Maj. Gen. Clayton Vogel of the Marine Corps a brief demonstration of their skills. On the morning of February 28, 1942, at an office in Los Angeles, the volunteers coded, transmitted, and decoded three-line messages filled with specialized military vocabulary. The messages were dictated in English, sent in Navajo over a field telephone, and written down in English as received. Impressed with the results, the Marines authorized a program that began with twenty-nine Navajo men.

Initially the Navajo recruits devised and memorized code words for more than 200 military terms (the vocabulary was later expanded to more than 450 words), creating a code that even fellow Navajos could not follow. The Navajo word for eagle, for example, is *atsá*, but in the code it meant "transport plane." *Chaa'* means "beaver," but for Navajo code talkers it meant "minesweeper." During the war, some 380 Navajo Marines serving in the Pacific participated in the classified Navajo Code Talker Program. They worked mainly in two-man teams, using walkie-talkies and field telephones to call in military maneuvers and report enemy movements. They took part in every

Two Navajo Marines operate a portable radio set
close behind the front lines, December 1943.
Solomon Islands. Photo by U.S. Marine Corps.

Marine assault, from Guadalcanal in 1942 to Okinawa in 1945, changing the code for each island campaign. The complex, monthlong op-
eration to capture the island of Iwo Jima was directed entirely by
orders communicated in Navajo code. By the war's end thousands of
messages had been transmitted, but the Japanese never succeeded in
breaking the code.

In the summer of 2001, Congress awarded Congressional Silver
Medals—the highest honor Congress can bestow on a citizen of the
United States—to the twenty-nine Navajo Marines who originally
developed the code.

Choctaws also served as code talkers in World War II, as did
seventeen Comanche servicemen. Meskwaki, Sioux, Crow, Hopi, and
Cree soldiers also took part. The Comanche men were recruited for

the U.S. Army Signal Corps to devise a top secret, 250-word code that would be incomprehensible to the German military. On June 6, 1944 (D-Day), they laid communications lines for Allied forces landing on the beaches of Normandy. Over the next eleven months, they participated in four other major campaigns, sending messages on troop movements, strength, and weaponry. These men received commendations from their commander, and in 1989 the French government awarded them the Chevalier de l'Ordre National du Mérite.

—MARY AHENAKEW

DO ALASKA NATIVES REALLY HAVE HUNDREDS OF WORDS FOR SNOW?

It is true that the Yup'ik and Inupiaq peoples of northern Alaska and the Inuit people of northern Canada have a seemingly unlimited number of words and phrases that describe types, textures, and amounts of snowfall. Many other words describe different conditions that exist when snow is on the ground. Yup'ik and Inupiaq are only two of Alaska's eleven culture groups, but in those languages single words can often express detailed descriptions.

The vast array of snow descriptions in Yup'ik and Inupiaq is possible largely because the languages are polysynthetic, meaning that entire sentences can be formed by a single word. Many different suffixes also can be added to a root word, such as *snow*, making it possible for the Yup'ik and Inupiaq to say in one word what an English speaker would need several words—perhaps even an entire sentence—to say.

Types of snowfall include such simple conditions as lightly falling snow, heavy wet snow, blowing snow, and others. Because Native peoples have always had to understand the land on which they live with an eye toward communal survival, it makes sense that weather would be closely monitored by indigenous peoples, particularly those in climates where changes in weather can be extreme. Describing a weather condition in detailed language—and adapting one's behavior to more easily live with it—is a practice common to many other Native peoples, including Native Hawaiians, who have countless words to describe rain (for example, rain that sweeps over the ocean to the islands; misty, cool rains of the valley regions; torrential downpours in the rain forests), an important feature of their tropical environment. Because snow is an important part of many Native Alaskan people's

environment (in northern Alaska, snow covers the ground for most of each year), the ability to describe the various kinds of snow was—and continues to be—crucial to their survival on the land.

Here is a list of a few of the different types of snow that have been described by Inuit people, in just one dialect, the Copper Inuit: *aniu* (good snow to make drinking water); *apiqqun* (first snow in autumn); *apun* (fallen snow); *aqilluqaq* (fresh soft snow); *mahak* (melting snow); *minguliq* (falling powdered snow); *natiruvik* (snow blowing along a surface); *patuqun* (frosty sparkling snow); *pukak* (sugar snow); *pukaraq* (fine sugar snow); *qaniaq* (light soft snow); *qanik* (snowflake); *qanniq* (falling snow in general); *qayuqhak* (snowdrift shaped by the wind, resembling a duck's head); and *ukharyuk, qimuyuk, aputtaaq* (snowbank).

—LIZ HILL AND NEMA MAGOVERN

DID INDIANS HAVE MATHEMATICS BEFORE CONTACT WITH EUROPEANS?

Yes. Native people used number systems long before contact with Europeans. American Indians developed decimal systems, as well as sequences based on the numbers five, ten, and twenty. Many Native languages also had words for the numbers one through ten. Inuit people of the subarctic regions, for example, counted to one hundred using their hands and feet. Two hands equals ten; the addition of one foot equals fifteen; the other foot brings the total to twenty. Twenty represents one person; one person plus five fingers equals twenty-five; and so on. Five people equal one hundred, which also represents one bundle, such as a bundle of sticks or animal skins.

The Maya of Mesoamerica are said to have developed the most sophisticated mathematical principles and applications of all the indigenous people of the Western Hemisphere. Numbers up to nineteen were written in combinations of bars, each of which had a value of five, and dots, each representing a value of one. "Head variant numerals," or portraits of the heads of Maya gods shown in profile, represented the number of each head's facial features or attributes. The Maya had three words for "twenty": *kal, may,* and *uinic,* the last of which was also the term for "human being." Multiples of twenty followed a regular sequence up to 380, after which came "one 400."

The Maya ceremonial calendar of 260 days is called the *tzolkin,* the Sequence of Days, the Sacred Almanac, or the Sacred Round. This calendar consists of a cycle of thirteen day numbers and a cycle of twenty day names. The day names are represented by glyphs. They also have a calendar of 365 days, which is referred to as the Vague Year because it does not preserve a precise alignment with the seasons over long periods. The Vague Year is made up of eighteen name

Inka quipu, a device used for recording statistics, ca. AD 1470. Chupaca, Peru.

Photo by NMAI Photo Services staff. 14/3866

months of twenty days each, with a residual period of five days. The Maya use both of these calendars to generate what is called the Calendar Round, which consists of 18,980 Calendar Round dates.

The Inka of the Andean regions kept statistics about crops, llamas, weapons, births, and deaths. These figures were recorded using *quipus*—knotted strings of different colors and lengths. The record keepers responsible for these tallies were called *quipu camayacs*, or rememberers. Each rememberer designed his own quipu, and the rememberers would get together to explain how their quipus were coded, so that the knotted strings could be interpreted by others. Quipus were not used for computation, but rather to record totals that had been obtained by using piles of grains, pebbles, or an abacus-like counting tray. The Inka used the decimal system and understood the abstract concept of zero, as did the Maya.

In North America the Pomo of the West Coast used stick counting and tying knots in string. The number of days it took to complete a journey was recorded by tying knots on a string. One knot represented one day, so the strings were called day counts. The stick system could be applied to compile records of large quantities and could involve the use of two different-sized sticks. Most tribes used the principles of addition and multiplication, but only some used subtraction and division.

—MARY AHENAKEW

BEFORE THE ARRIVAL OF FORMAL SCHOOLS, HOW WERE INDIAN CHILDREN TAUGHT?

Traditionally, the entire community was responsible for educating Native children. Parents, grandparents, relatives, elders, clan members, and societies that hold knowledge reserved only for members transmitted the everyday skills, history, beliefs, and social mores of the tribe. Unlike those of Euro-Americans, many Native social structures were matrilineal and matrilocal, meaning that heritage was traced through the mother. In horticultural societies, such as the Pueblo and Haudenosaunee (Iroquois) communities, responsibility for educating and disciplining the children fell to the first male blood relative in the mother's clan, usually her brother, the children's maternal uncle. In addition, tribal elders were highly respected as wisdom keepers and knowledge bearers. They ensured that community history, values, and cultural information were passed to future generations. Elders retain this highly regarded position today. While formal schooling and the nuclear family play major roles in Native education today, clan and community still perform a significant function as teachers.

Before European contact, Native children were taught the skills necessary to fill their social roles as adults. Young boys learned tracking, hunting, fishing, and farming methods, observational skills, and how to increase their physical abilities. The girls learned how to care for the home and children, prepare food, and create utensils such as pottery and baskets. Children would be given small replicas of tools they would need as adults to play and practice with, such as a bow and arrow, a doll, or a mortar and pestle. Both boys and girls were given religious training in the spiritual beliefs and the cosmological world view of their people. Young people also gained privi-

leged knowledge through induction into certain medicine, warrior, or other societies. Only those who were members of the society were privy to its secrets. A young person could learn through apprenticeship as well. A holy or medicine person would sense that a particular youth was suited—either by temperament, intelligence, or intuitiveness—to bear the medicine, or holy knowledge, of his or her people.

Children learned by listening, observing, and doing. They were instructed to analyze the world around them, the behavior of the animals, the changing of the weather. Their parents and other teachers encouraged them through example and positive and negative reinforcement, but harsh punishment was not a characteristic of Native education. As children grew older, they could seek answers to specific questions through certain rituals, such as vision quests. Learning was a lifelong process. One did not reach the position of an esteemed elder until very late in life.

With the arrival of Europeans came Jesuit missionaries and Protestant ministers, who established mission schools in the 1600s and 1700s to provide training in religion, the English language, and the industrial arts. Newcomers viewed a "proper" education as a way of bringing Native people out of their supposedly primitive and heathenish conditions into the light of "civilization." Schools tended to replace Native values of sharing and cooperation with a European emphasis on individualism and competition, which threatened to fray the fabric of community.

The history of Native education under U.S. and Canadian policies has been a tragic one. Government and religious schools eroded traditional values and greatly contributed to the loss of many Native languages. From the 1880s to the 1920s (to the 1970s in Canada), children who were forcibly removed from their families and placed in boarding schools faced humiliation and despair. The quality of Indian education continues to be an issue today. Since the 1970s, more and more tribes have reclaimed their children's futures by creating tribal education departments, establishing their own schools, and becoming more involved in curriculum development for students both on and off the reservation.

Family and community continue to play a major role in the education and acculturation of children. Hundreds of tribally operated Head Start programs, elementary schools, and high schools teach traditional languages and cultural values together with reading, writing, and math. Native Americans, along with Hispanics, remain statistically unsuccessful: high school dropout rates are high and attainment

Navajo silversmith at work, with a young girl looking on, ca. 1915. Arizona.

Photo by Carl Moon. N31720

of college degrees low. But the numbers have improved during the past twenty years, and Native people will continue to battle whenever their children's futures are at stake.

—ARWEN NUTTALL

WHAT ARE KACHINA DOLLS? WHAT ARE THEY USED FOR?

Kachina, or *katsina*, dolls are not toys. They are intended for young people, but unlike toys, these special objects are a serious and important part of a young person's education in the Hopi, Zuni, and other Pueblo communities of the Southwest.

For the Hopi people of Arizona, katsina dolls—three-dimensional carved and painted cottonwood figures—are seen as physical representations of the *katsinam,* deities that traditionally come to stay in Hopi villages for six months of the year. Parents, grandparents, and other relatives give katsinas to children as part of their training, so they can learn about the different katsinam, which the Hopi and other Pueblo people recognize in many ceremonies and dances. There are literally several hundred katsinam—and all are central to Hopi social and ceremonial life.

It is believed that some of the katsinam came to the Hopi people from other pueblos in the Southwest—in particular, the Pueblo of Zuni in New Mexico. Katsinam, who may embody male or female characteristics, represent the beings that make up the natural world, such as plants (corn), insects, animals (deer, wolf, antelope), and birds (eagle, owl). Some display human traits, such as humor, leadership, and discipline.

The Hopi people believe that the katsinam arrive in their villages in human form at the solstice in late December and stay until July. During this time the katsinam serve as messengers between the temporal and spiritual worlds, carrying the prayers of the Hopi people to the gods. They also are said to have supernatural powers—for example, they can control the weather by bringing rain for crops. During social dances and ceremonies, the katsinam, embodied by

Scott Secakuku (Hopi) carves a katsina doll. A finished doll stands beside him, 2001. Phoenix, Arizona.

Photo © 2003 John Harrington (Siletz) and the National Museum of the American Indian.

men in masks, guide various community activities. All Hopi people belong to either the Katsina or Powamuy ritual societies.

One of the most famous of the katsinam is the Kokopelli, a Hopi fertility god whose present-day form is that of a carefree, playful, humpbacked flautist. One sees Kokopelli in many advertisements, on signs, and emblazoned on commercial sale items in the American Southwest. Other katsinam well known to non-Natives include the Koshari and Mudhead, who have the role of clowns.

In the book *Meet Mindy, a Native Girl from the Southwest* (2003), Mindy Secakuku, a contemporary Hopi girl who spends a lot of time on the Hopi Reservation, explains, "The katsinam bring gifts to children who have been good. These gifts can be fruit or other food, or musical instruments like rattles, drums, or dancing sticks. A katsina may give a girl a very special gift of a miniature doll that looks like it, called *tihu*. You know you've been good when you get a katsina doll!"

—LIZ HILL

WHY DID THE U.S. GOVERNMENT FORCE INDIAN CHILDREN INTO BOARDING SCHOOLS?

White missionaries and other reformers in the nineteenth and early twentieth centuries were certain that their way of thinking and being was the one right way. They felt honor bound to "civilize" the supposedly primitive peoples on whose land they had settled, and they knew that they needed to start with the impressionable minds of children. The prevailing concept was "kill the Indian, save the man." So, beginning in earnest in the 1870s, they established boarding schools. Following government policy they took children—sometimes with the parents' consent and sometimes by force—and sent them to boarding schools as far away from their homes as possible, to keep the children from running away. During summer vacations the children were allowed to go home if the parents came for them or sent enough money for train fare. If a child had poor parents, that child often went many years without contact with his or her people.

The boarding-school system, which included schools on reservations as well as day schools, emphasized manual labor and conformity to late nineteenth-century Euro-American values. Boys learned carpentry, blacksmithing, gardening, and farming. Girls worked in the laundry, sewed, and helped cook the meals. Academic courses included history, math, spelling, reading, writing, and geography. Daily schedules were strictly regulated, independent action was discouraged, and children were harshly punished for speaking any language other than English.

By the 1930s the efforts of reformers, together with changes in the public education system, had led to the closing of nearly all Indian boarding schools in the United States, but in Canada, most government-

Navajo pupils at Albuquerque Indian School,
1904. Albuquerque, New Mexico.

N26622

and church-run residential schools continued well into the 1970s. On
both sides of the border, survivors of the system remember their experiences. At a conference held at Trent University in Ontario in 2003,
former boarding-school students told of rapes by adults, beatings given
for the slightest infraction of rules, and lack of proper food. In one
case, the government took a student named Alan from his family in
Oklahoma at the age of four. He was housed in a large dormitory for
boys where he was sexually abused nightly by bigger boys. "I used to
cry and cry," he said.

—GEORGETTA STONEFISH RYAN

This photo of American Indian students in 1909 dressed for the roles of Priscilla Alden and Myles Standish for the play *Captain of Plymouth* at the Carlisle Indian Industrial School demonstrates how thoroughly Anglo-European values permeated the school's curricula.

Photo courtesy of the Cumberland County Historical Society, Carlisle, Pennsylvania.

WHAT ARE TRIBAL COLLEGES?

As the era of "self-determination" took hold in the 1970s, Native people of the United States gained more meaningful control of federal programs affecting their communities. Tribal governments began to take greater charge of their own destinies, including the education of their citizens. Recognizing the failure of the federal government's efforts to provide adequate educational opportunities, Indian peoples began to take new approaches to educating their children, and groundbreaking Indian education legislation was passed by Congress. A natural outgrowth of self-determination was the establishment of American Indian tribal colleges.

North America's thirty-two tribal colleges are institutions of postsecondary learning that primarily serve the educational needs of Native students. For the most part, they are chartered and administered by tribal governments. Most are located on reservations, with a few notable exceptions. In 2003 some 60 percent of all Native students (some thirty thousand) attended tribal colleges. And, although people of all backgrounds and ethnicities are welcome to enroll at tribal colleges, students tend to be primarily American Indian. Many of the colleges offer two-year associate degrees and certificates, but ten also offer baccalaureate degrees. A few offer master's degrees in leadership.

The Navajo Nation established the first tribal college in 1968, calling it Navajo Community College. Some other well-known tribal colleges include Haskell Indian Nations University in Lawrence, Kansas; the Institute of American Indian Arts in Santa Fe, New Mexico; and United Tribes Technical College in Bismarck, North Dakota.

Tribal colleges receive little or no funding from local or state

governments. They must rely upon endowments and support from the federal government. Founded in 1972, the American Indian Higher Education Consortium (AIHEC) lobbies the U.S. Congress on behalf of tribal colleges and works to find continued financial support through federal government sources. The American Indian College Fund, established in 1989 by tribal colleges, has as its mission to raise private and foundation monies for tribal colleges and universities. Two executive orders, the first signed by President Bill Clinton in 1996, and the second by President George W. Bush in 2002, affirm the importance of tribal colleges to Indian education at all levels, from preschool to post-graduate.

Curricula vary widely in tribal colleges, although all of them offer courses that teach their tribes' languages, histories, and cultures, together with a variety of courses geared toward developing professional skills useful for future work in tribal communities.

In her testimony to the U.S. Senate Committee on Indian Affairs in February 1999, Janine Pease-Pretty on Top (Crow), then the president of AIHEC and former president of Little Big Horn College, had this to say: "These vital institutions have come to represent the most significant development in American Indian educational history, promoting achievement among students who most likely would never know educational success."

—LIZ HILL

LOVE AND
MARRIAGE

How were traditional Native romances conducted? Is it the same today?

In traditional Native American societies, a relationship between a man and a woman was a serious matter. It was perhaps not what contemporary Americans might consider a "romance," an intensely felt, amorous liaison between two people that may or may not lead to marriage. Little time was available in traditional Native societies for what was probably considered frivolous or adolescent behavior (in fact, until recently, casual unions were frowned upon in most Native communities).

Why? Wherever Native peoples lived—on the Great Plains, in the eastern and northern woodlands, in the Arctic, or in the deserts—life could be precarious. Native people struggled just to stay alive, feed their families, and provide themselves with basic necessities under sometimes extremely challenging conditions. The union of two people in what today we call marriage—an institution that was regulated for Native people by Christianity and other Western value systems—was a momentous undertaking in any Native community, one that was seen as a way to enhance family standings in the community or to establish other positive relationships—for example, trade—with a neighboring group. Parents were closely involved in choosing suitable partners for their sons and daughters, with an eye toward partnerships that would benefit both families. Arranged marriages were common in many Native cultures, and could be negotiated even before the young people were born. Courtship was monitored.

Because families considered marriage a means of raising their status in the community, people with greater means were expected to aid the less fortunate. This arrangement sometimes meant that wealthy men took more than one wife (the women might be sis-

Kiowa drawing of a courting scene, with five couples wrapped in blankets, 1875–1877. Fort Marion, St. Augustine, Florida.

Smithsonian Institution National Anthropological Archives. 08547623

ters) and, sometimes, that women married several men who were brothers.

Native people today conduct their romances in a variety of ways. Romances leading to marriage outside one's tribe and with people of other races have become as commonplace for Native peoples as for other Americans, Canadians, Native Hawaiians, or Central and South Americans. Some traditions, however, hold fast for some tribes, especially taboos against marriage between two people of the same clan. This convention protects a long-standing way of identifying family lineages.

—LIZ HILL

How can I have a traditional Native American wedding?

No one traditional way of getting married exists for Native Americans. Ceremonies and celebrations varied greatly from tribe to tribe, although tribes located near one another often had similar practices. Marriage in most Native American societies was less a matter of romance than of economics and tribal requirements for steady relationships. People from the same clan didn't usually marry, but since Native communities were much more insular than they are today, most people married within their tribe.

Families, often elder women relatives, usually arranged or approved the union of a young woman and man. It was seen as a situation that could benefit both families. Prearranged marriages were not always embraced by the young people, but a refusal to marry the family's choice could be detrimental to the tribe. In the Southwest the Hopi and Navajo required the groom's family to pay a bride's price, or dowry, and the bride's family reciprocated with equal gifts.

Tlingit people in southeastern Alaska separate themselves into two groups—the Eagles and the Ravens, with inheritance passed through the mother's clan. Traditionally, it was required that someone born an Eagle could marry only a Raven, and vice versa. Traditional rules have relaxed a great deal, but many Tlingits today believe that it is still best to marry someone of the opposite group. Some Iroquois tribes and a few western tribes also keep their marriage traditions alive. Haudenosaunee (Iroquois) families exchange baskets. Hopi uncles of the groom weave cotton robes for the bride, and Hopi wedding participants dust their faces with cornmeal, which is considered sacred. The Cherokee use a two-spigot vase, from which the bride

and groom drink, and the Plains tribes sometimes wrap a blanket around the bride and groom and tie a knot.

Today American Indians may get married also by Christian clergy, a judge, or at city hall. If you are Native American, some of the traditions are applicable, but any wedding, whether Native or non-Native, should be held in high esteem and be appropriate for the couple.

—NEMA MAGOVERN

How Have Native Americans Viewed Homosexuality?

Before sustained contact with Europeans in the years before 1492, the concept of homosexuality did not exist among Native cultures—at least not according to the contemporary definition of the term, which has more to do with sexual behaviors than it does with gender differences and established roles in the community. Before the twentieth century a number of Native cultures accepted men and women who "crossed genders," effectively taking on the attributes of the opposite sex, most commonly in their style of dress and in their village duties and responsibilities.

The Native individuals who chose to live their lives as members of the opposite sex were not what contemporary mainstream society might define as homosexuals, transvestites, or transsexuals. Some cultures considered these Native individuals special, believing them to be an entirely different gender—someone who had a third, fourth, or more genders in one body. One of the most well-known and documented of these individuals was We'wha (1849–1896), a Zuni man who lived out his life as a woman—dressing in women's clothes and performing the daily tasks of a Zuni woman. We'wha was a much-valued and loved member of his community. In 1886 he visited Washington, D.C., as an official representative of his people. While there, he danced at the National Theater before an audience that included President Grover Cleveland (whom he subsequently met) and demonstrated the weaving techniques of the Zuni people at the Smithsonian Institution. When he died, his community widely mourned his passing.

The French word *berdache*, which was first used by the Jesuits when they observed men in women's dress among the Iroquois, has

been the word most widely used to describe Native individuals who crossed genders. Today the preferred term of many Native people is *two-spirit*, a person who possesses both the male and female spirits. Will Roscoe, author of *The Zuni Man-Woman* (1991) has noted that two-spirit people and the acceptance of them were once widespread among more than 155 tribes.

In *Native America in the Twentieth Century* (1996), Lakota anthropologist Beatrice Medicine wrote, "In sum, it is apparent that aboriginal people in North America were more tolerant than many other cultures of gender variation. . . . However, in many Native communities, there seems to be an emerging intolerance which may mirror that of Anglo society. Still, a tolerance is evident. There is a strong respect for persons and their individual autonomy, despite any cross-gender orientation."

—LIZ HILL

DID ANY INDIAN GROUPS PRACTICE POLYGAMY?

Some groups did practice polygamy, while others did not. *Polygamy* is usually defined as having more than one wife. Before contact with Europeans, the concept of marriage differed among various indigenous peoples.

In most eastern woodland cultures, a man lived with his wife's family in a large wooden longhouse. When other female siblings married, their husbands moved in with them. The Apache, Navajo, Mi'kmaq, and other tribes across North America followed the same pattern. Men in the community would take responsibility for supporting sisters, daughters, mothers, and other female family members if tragedy struck a male provider. But all the women in one family were usually not the "wives" of the lone man.

Father Andrew White, one of the Jesuit priests who came in 1634 to what is today Maryland, used every available opportunity to convert the Native people he encountered to the Catholic faith. When Kittamaqua, the *tayac*, or tribal leader, of the Piscataway Confederacy, fell ill, his healers were unable to cure him. Father White wrote in his journal that he administered a "powder of known efficacy" to the tayac, which effected what must have seemed to Kittamaqua and his people a miraculous cure. The tayac submitted to baptism, because his remarkable recovery proved to him the power of the priest's God. As a condition of being baptized, wrote Father White, Kittamaqua "put away all wives but one." Since no mention is made of the tayac's having children by these other "wives," Father White may have mistaken a single wife's female relatives for multiple wives.

In some of the northern Plains and Plateau communities, marriages could be either monogamous or polygamous. It has been esti-

mated that at one time about 20 percent of marriages in these regions included more than one wife. Leading families in a community carried responsibilities of hosting and labor that encouraged the taking of multiple spouses. Most often, sisters would marry one man, who could provide for them both. In contrast, the Haudenosaunee (Iroquois) tribes in the Northeast and the southwestern Pueblo peoples tended to have only one spouse at a time. But no matter what the formal arrangements between individuals, the primary purpose of family alliances was to make sure orphans were cared for and to maintain the strength and stability of the community as a whole.

—RICO NEWMAN

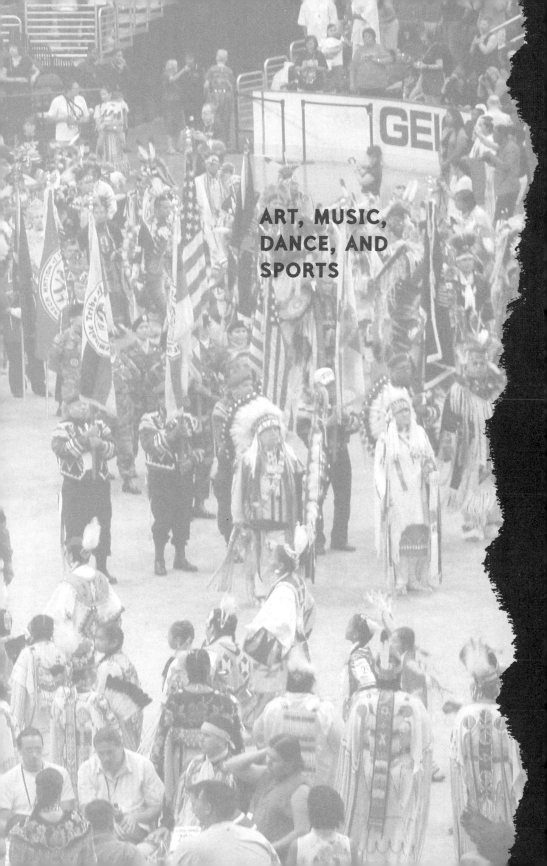

ART, MUSIC,
DANCE, AND
SPORTS

WHAT WAS THE FIRST GAME EVER PLAYED WITH RUBBER BALLS?

A precursor of the modern game of basketball was the first game ever played with rubber balls, which were invented in Meso-america thousands of years ago. Along with other games, it was played among the Olmec people—whose civilization flourished in Mesoamerica between 1700 BC and AD 400—and among the Aztec (who called their game *tlachiti*), the Maya, and other indigenous peoples of the region. Today's soccer, baseball, football, and the modern game of basketball (which was invented in 1891 by James Naismith, a teacher in Springfield, Massachusetts) all have their origins in Mesoamerican ball games.

The Mesoamerican ball game was for boys and men of all social classes. Teams played against one another during feast days. The object of the game was for the player to hit a rubber ball with his hips or buttocks into the opposing team's end zone or into one of the stone or wooden hoops that protruded from the sides of the courts. The game was so popular that remnants of hundreds of ball courts have been found from Bolivia to Arizona, and in parts of the Caribbean.

Rubber was a significant invention of the indigenous peoples of the Americas. The Olmec—who were even known as the Rubber People by other tribes—were the first people in the world to produce rubber from latex, a sap that comes from the native *Hevea brasiliensis*, or rubber tree, found in Mesoamerica and along the Amazon River in South America. Latex was collected from the rubber trees, cleaned, and then cured with smoke from a fire made with palm nuts. After the latex was mixed with sulfur, the naturally bad odor of the latex disappeared, its stickiness was eliminated, and the final product became like the rubber we know today: hardy and impervious to mois-

ture. Centuries later, in 1839, the process, known as vulcanization, was rediscovered by the American inventor Charles Goodyear.

The Maya people of Central America and the Quechua people of South America were also known for their use of rubber products. Rubber had a role in a variety of domestic and utilitarian items, including food and water containers, rubber ropes, and clothing, such as raincoats and footgear.

During his second voyage to the Americas in 1493–1496, Christopher Columbus reputedly became the first European to see rubber balls, a fact that was documented by Antonio de Herrera y Tordesillas, a historian serving in the court of King Phillip II of Spain. Ironically, the use of rubber was not at all popular in Europe until the invention of rubber tires in the late 1890s. For the first explorers in the Americas, rubber was easily overlooked in their insatiable quest for precious metals, such as gold and silver, and cash crops such as tobacco.

—LIZ HILL

DID ALL TRIBES HAVE TOTEM POLES? DOES ANYONE STILL CARVE THEM?

Native people along the North Pacific Coast from present-day Washington State to Alaska have a long history of intricately carving cedar logs with images of people, animals, and characters from oral narratives. The carvings are most often clan symbols— Raven, Bear, Eagle, or Killer Whale, for example—and they tell of supernatural events, journeys to other worlds, and community or family histories. In relating its story, a finished pole can reach a height of forty or more feet. There are many kinds of totem poles: poles for the entrance of a house, poles that honor a person who has died, poles that tell stories, and poles that welcome people to a school or community center.

Over time, totem poles eventually disintegrate and return to the earth. As a result, no one knows when the practice of carving them began. The estimated ages of the oldest existing poles are between 100 and 150 years. Figures similar to those carved on the wood poles also have been found on stone surfaces. This finding suggests that the practice of carving has persisted on the North Pacific Coast for several millennia.

When a potlatch is held, the sponsoring family may have a totem pole erected to commemorate the occasion. A potlatch is a celebration that can take many forms, but usually the hosts invite a large group, provide an abundant feast, and give each participant gifts. The more the hosts give away, the more honor they bring to themselves. In the 1880s, Canadian church and government officials interpreted the potlatch as a negative influence that encouraged wastefulness, so the potlatch was outlawed in Canada from the 1880s to the 1950s. Although potlatches were still held in many communities during the ban, the

tradition—together with totem pole carving—suffered a decline. Today Native communities along the North Pacific Coast have revived potlatches, seeing them as an integral connection to their ancestors.

Among the many contemporary Native totem pole carvers along the North Pacific Coast, a group from the Lummi Nation of Washington State called the House of Tears Carvers believes that totem poles can be a means of national commemoration and healing. One carver suggests that carving brings out both happiness and sadness. When a tree is cut, it is sad, and the carvers offer gifts to honor and thank the cedar. When the carvers are finished, they cry with joy at what they have brought forth from the spirit of the tree.

In 2002 the Lummi carvers erected a totem pole called *The Healing Pole* in the Sterling Forest, about sixty miles north of Manhattan. It was named to help bring about resolution to the grief of families and communities following the attack on the World Trade Center towers on September 11, 2001.

Although totem poles today are carved almost exclusively by the people of the North Pacific Coast, the practice of carving figures in trees and stone has a long history in Native cultures throughout the Americas. The Lenni Lenape, Piscataway, Powhatan, Haudenosaunee (Iroquois), and many other eastern and southern tribes carved what were called "living faces" in trees.

Kaats totem pole, in the National Museum of the American Indian, tells the story of Kaats, the Bear Hunter. For more information on this totem pole see page 146. Nathan P. Jackson (Tlingit), Stephen P. Jackson (Tlingit), and Dorica R. Jackson, 2004. Saxman, Alaska. NMAI museum commission, 2004.

Photo by Ernest Amoroso. 26/3856

> While most people believe that the "lowest person on the to-
> tem pole" is the least esteemed, totem carvers know that the fig-
> ure at the bottom of the pole holds a position of great honor.

And the pre-Contact cultures of Mesoamerica and South America carved entire stories on the walls of their stone palaces and temples.

Totem poles have differing purposes and hold complex meanings. Many people think that totem poles are religious objects, but the communities that carve them have never worshipped them. Rather, totem poles tell stories of family, clan, and community, linking people with their ancestors and their origins.

—RICO NEWMAN

WHAT DID INDIANS USE FOR PAINT AND DYE?

From earliest times, Native Americans have used their surroundings as a source of color. Indigenous rocks, clays, plants, and flowers have been transformed into paints and dye that reflect the full spectrum of natural hues. By creating paintings on ceramics and hide as well as dyeing yarn and grasses, Indian people have found ways to decorate everyday and ritual objects.

In northeastern North America the Mi'kmaq used pollen to dye splints for baskets, and the Mohegan used potatoes to stamp designs. In the Southeast the Cherokee used bloodroot, a tiny plant with white flowers that grows in wooded areas, to make different shades of rose and reddish brown. Walnut root and yellow root also provided natural dyes. The Choctaw of Mississippi wove colorful baskets of native river cane.

On the coast of the Mar del Sur, in present-day Mexico, the Chontales made a red dye called cochineal, or *grana cochinilla*, from tiny mites that live on cacti. After the arrival of the Spanish, dyeing became a business for the Native people in the mountainous part of the region. The famous red coats of the eighteenth-century English infantry were dyed with cochineal.

The tribes of the Great Plains were the masters of adornment. Traditional clothing included shirts, leggings, moccasins, dresses, and buffalo robes. From clothing to tipis, hide objects were decorated with meaningful, often personal, designs and pictographs. Hide painting was done on buffalo robes, tipi covers, and clothing. Iron-laden earth clays yielded rich paints of brown, red, and yellow. Scoops of black earth were used for dark colors. The clays were pulverized in stone mortars and then made sticky by glue from plants. Both men

A bloodroot flower growing in the forest landscape at the National Museum of the American Indian. The roots and stems of the bloodroot are used to create a reddish-brown or rose-colored dye.

Photo by Hayes P. Lavis.

and women were artists. Men painted robes, shirts, shields, and tipis. Women painted geometric figures and did quillwork and beadwork.

In southwestern North America local flora provided a wealth of color possibilities. The Navajo weave beautiful rugs and blankets, using different colors of wool from various breeds of sheep. For dyes, they use indigo (the oldest of all dye plants) to create a deep blue, rabbitbrush to make yellow, sagebrush to produce a muddy green or off-brown, and mahogany roots to yield orange-red, deep purple, or lavender. Soil, climate, and rainfall all affect the colors that the plants produce. Many weavers today use dyes available in stores, but some still work with indigenous plants, which they harvest, soak, ferment, and dry until they are exactly the right color for their yarn, clay, grasses, or hide.

—NEMA MAGOVERN

WHAT IS A TOM-TOM DRUM?

Native Americans throughout the Western Hemisphere use many different shapes and sizes of drums made from a variety of materials, but no Native people call these drums *tom-toms*. It is not clear when the word *tom-tom* began to be used in connection with Native American drums. The term probably originated in the Hindi language (of India). Webster's online dictionary notes that the word *tom-tom* was first used in popular English literature sometime before 1894. Of course, non-Native literary and screen writers later used it to describe Native American drums.

To understand Native American drums, it is first important to learn about some of the cultural meanings associated with them. Imagine a warm summer evening at an outdoor arena, where Native Americans from many tribes are taking part in a powwow. They have already witnessed many dances and songs. Now the emcee calls for a Round Dance, a social dance in which the participants form a circle that symbolizes unity, connectedness, and friendship among them. The drum group, several men who sit around the edge of a large, circular drum, each with his own drumstick, begins a soft beat with a deliberate and steady long-short rhythm. To the Native Americans in the audience, the drum is the heartbeat of the earth, the people, and this event. The rhythm reaches into the center of their beings and they are compelled to dance, join in, and celebrate this expression of their cultural identities. As the dance continues, the drummers carry on their pulsing rhythm, now louder, now softer. As the volume and intensity of the drumming and singing grow, so do the emotions of the dancers. The drum and its rhythms are essential to the successful completion of cultural gatherings such as powwows throughout Indian Country.

A drum group at the National Powwow,
August 14, 2005. Washington, D.C.

Photo by Cindy Frankenburg.

A powwow is but one type among hundreds of Native American events that include music and drums. Drums are used at various social gatherings and in many ceremonies. Among Native Americans, drums are held in respect no matter where they come from or what events they are used for. In some settings, drums are considered to be living spiritual entities. They are given names and offerings; they are ritually fed and purified with the smoke of sacred plants. Drums are often painted or decorated with symbols of significance to the people who use the drum. A person is sometimes given the responsibility of caring for the drum, and individuals and families sometimes own drums that they pass along from generation to generation.

Native American drums are made from many different materials, including wood, clay, and even modern synthetic materials. Some drums have two heads and some have one, usually made of animal hides. Most drums are played by one person, but some of the big drums are played by many individuals at the same time.

To Native Americans, drums are sacred, and humans have a spiritual and emotional connection to them. Drums play an important part throughout the lives of individuals and are an element that binds and preserves the cultures of Native communities.

—EDWIN SCHUPMAN

DO INDIANS PLAY ANYTHING BUT DRUMS AND FLUTES?

Drums and flutes are integral to Native music throughout the Western Hemisphere, but many other types of instruments are common. Rattles, bells, striking sticks, rasps, and whistles also can be an important part of social dances and religious ceremonies. Rattles are made of materials such as turtle shell, animal horn, gourds, rawhide, and elm bark. The material is shaped to form a hollow vessel and filled with seeds, gravel, or pebbles to create the rattle sound. Other materials, such as deer dewclaws, buffalo hooves, animal knucklebones, or seashells can be strung together to create a rattling sound. Handles are made of wood or bone, and many rattles are decorated with beads, porcupine quills, feathers, horsehair.

The rasp consists of a stick of hard wood, notched like a saw, or a grooved dried gourd over which a smaller stick is rubbed back and forth, creating a rhythm. Some tribes have stringed instruments such as fiddles. The Seri of Mesoamerica have a one-string, box-shaped fiddle, and the Apache a one- or two-stringed violin, also called a fiddle. The Apache fiddle is played with a bow made from the century plant stalk and one or two horsehair strings. The Quechua and Aymara people of the Andes have a guitarlike instrument called a *charango*, which is made from the armor of an armadillo.

Depending on the region, trumpets or horns were made from materials such as bamboo, conch shells, clay, wood, the tail of the armadillo, or tree bark. Some instruments were used for hunting. A horn made from bark was used by northeastern tribes to attract moose, and whistles made from wood or animal bone were used to call game. Some whistles were created especially to scare birds away from vegetable gardens.

Singer, songwriter, musician, actor, and playwright Arigon Starr (Kickapoo/Creek) in her one-woman play, *The Red Road*. National Museum of the American Indian, August 5, 2006. Washington, D.C.

Photo by Katherine Fogden (Mohawk).

In addition to playing these traditional instruments, contemporary Native people—as classical, jazz, rock, folk, and pop musicians—play many other kinds of instruments. Some Native American communities have also adapted non-Native instruments and musical styles, making them part of their own contemporary cultural expressions. In southern Arizona, for example, musicians of the Akimel O'odham and Tohono O'odham tribes perform a style of music known as *Waila* or *Chicken Scratch* music, which originated when a European priest brought an accordion to the local mission. Chicken Scratch is performed at community events by ensembles that include instruments such as violins, accordions, guitars, bass guitars, drums, saxophones, and trumpets. This distinct style features Native American adaptations of Latin American polkas, two-steps, and *cumbias,* a folk dance that originated in Colombia. As people who are fully engaged in the contemporary world, American Indian musicians see few limits on their creativity.

—MARY AHENAKEW AND EDWIN SCHUPMAN

Do Indians Chant?

No. Native Americans throughout the Western Hemisphere sing, but it is not accurate to refer to Native American singing as chant. Chant is described in *The Harvard Dictionary of Music* (2003) as a term that applies particularly to the liturgical music of the Christian churches. Non-Natives later used the word to describe Native singing, without really understanding how Native people themselves conceptualized the singing. Since the phrase *Indian chants* found its way into America's descriptive vocabulary, it has become embedded and difficult to counter. It has been reinforced by movie scripts, popular novels, television, and even music textbooks. The truth, however, is much richer than the one phrase implies.

According to Native American belief systems, music is intimately connected to everyday life and, especially, to the spiritual lives of Native peoples. Sacred music is an essential part of ceremonies and other important traditional activities. Social music is performed for personal enjoyment, at social events such as community or family celebrations, or as accompaniment to social dances. The idea of music for art's sake is not part of traditional Native thinking. Although singing is sometimes used as a form of artistic expression, there was no such thing historically as attending a concert of Native American music. Indeed, in most Native languages no words mean *music* in the sense that we know the word today. Instead, music and singing are linked to their many functions in Native cultures.

Song is the most common form of traditional Native American music. Frequently accompanied by various drums, rattles, and other percussive instruments, songs are sung at many different kinds of events for a wide variety of purposes. Sacred songs are considered to have a

power of their own, and they help Native people communicate within the spiritual universe. Sacred songs are sung by people such as traditional healers and participants in many types of ceremonies. They are used, for example, when seeking help from the spirit world with a problem, for success in hunting or fishing, during times of mourning, when honoring someone, or when praying for the well-being of one's family or community. Sacred songs are often considered gifts from the Creator, and it is believed that many of them originated long ago in powerful dreams or visions. In the Native way of thinking, such songs must always be treated respectfully because of their power. They can be harmful if misused, and they are only sung by people who have the appropriate cultural authority.

Native American singers use their voices in many expressive ways. Depending on the context, songs are sung solo or in groups, in unison, multipart, and even call-and-response textures. Some are peaceful and introspective, while others are forceful and dynamic. Some songs are sung only by men, some only by women, and some by both. Certain styles call for singing in a very high vocal range, while others are low. Occasionally singers express themselves and the cultural meaning of their music by quivering their voices, imitating animal noises, yelling, and making other special sounds. Sometimes the songs include words, either in the Native language or English, and other times they are just syllables, sometimes referred to as vocables.

The word *chant* belongs most appropriately to non-Native cultures and times. The unique world of Native American vocal music is richly varied, steeped in traditions, and an essential element of Native identity and cultural continuity.

—EDWIN SCHUPMAN

ISN'T A POWWOW A BIG MEETING OF LEADERS?

The meaning of the word *powwow* comes from the Algonquian term *pau-wau*; it refers to curing or healing ceremonies. The word was quickly adapted to the English language to refer to any Indian gathering, or it is used as a verb, meaning "to confer in council." To Native people, however, the word *powwow* came to signify important tribal or intertribal gatherings, fairs, and celebrations, featuring singing and social dancing for people of all ages.

Powwows are most often large, intertribal celebrations, yet they represent much more to Native people—they are a dynamic way of life that connects communities; they provide a sense of identity and pride, and offer a creative outlet for dancing, singing, cooking, beadwork, regalia making, and more. Although some community-based powwows are strictly traditional, most are large, intertribal, competition events that draw hundreds of dancers and thousands of spectators over two or three days and nights. Most powwows in the United States and Canada are held in the summer months. Traditionally powwows were held outdoors, but today many are held in large gymnasiums or sports arenas. Some of the largest include Schemitzun in Connecticut, Gathering of Nations in Albuquerque, New Mexico, and the Canadian Aboriginal Festival Powwow, held each year in the Toronto SkyDome.

Although powwows have changed over time, many aspects of powwows today have origins in the ceremonial war dances of the Great Plains. Sacred ceremonies of the Osage, Ponca, Kaw, Omaha, and Pawnee tribes, which are practiced today, form the basis of a powwow. Created in the 1950s, many of the Head Staff positions in the powwow arena today can be traced to the ceremonial offices held by tribal warriors. The role of the Arena Director, for example, evolved from that of

Grand Entry at the National Powwow, August 14, 2005. Washington, D.C.

Photo by Cindy Frankenburg.

the traditional Whip Men of Plains dance societies. The Whip Men were the first to respond to the call for dancers, encouraging others to rise and, when necessary, using their ceremonial whips on dancers' legs to get their attention.

As its origins show, a powwow can be viewed as a gathering of leaders. Contemporary powwows do bring together tribal leaders and tribal council leaders as well as many Native color guards and veterans, all of whom have proven their bravery and leadership by serving their country. These highly respected people often lead Grand Entry, the colorful procession of Native color guards, veterans, tribal leaders, pageant princesses, and dancers that takes place every morning and evening.

A powwow today is many things. It does bring together Native leaders, but it is largely a celebratory gathering where Native people can express themselves. Perhaps most importantly, powwows represent cultural survival and the ability to maintain Native identity into the twenty-first century.

—TANYA THRASHER

WHAT ARE LEDGER DRAWINGS?

aper became available to Plains Indians in the mid-nineteenth century, replacing hide as the standard surface for decoration and record keeping. Some Indian people drew on plain paper, but most people used the pages of lined ledger books bought from European traders, which may have been the first paper widely available in the West. Artists also used paper—often printed with agency letterhead—that Bureau of Indian Affairs agents had thrown away.

Pre-reservation art depicted battles, heroic deeds, buffalo hunts, the capture of horses, and other important aspects of tribal life. Reservation art showed a quieter time: social scenes, camp life, courting scenes, and dancing figures. Other artists during the reservation period preserved histories, cultural practices, and legends. In the late 1800s artists sold their ledger drawings to non-Natives by omitting the gorier details that could remind the buyers of tragedies, thus becoming the first Native commercial artists.

From 1875 to 1878 the U.S. Army arrested and incarcerated seventy-two Kiowa, Cheyenne, Arapaho, Caddo, and Comanche people at Fort Marion, in St. Augustine, Florida. Under Lt. Richard H. Pratt, the army provided the prisoners with pencils, crayons, pens, watercolors, ledger books, autograph booklets, and sketchbooks. The prisoners were encouraged to record their memories and recent experiences in souvenir booklets for visitors. The Comanche, Caddo, and two Arapaho prisoners did not draw, nor did the one woman. So at Fort Marion, as elsewhere, men drew or painted the world that they had known: hunts, raiding parties, and battles.

—GEORGETTA STONEFISH RYAN

Etahdleuh (1856–1888). Ledger drawing of two
mounted men, wearing finery, 1880. The horse
wears a Spanish-style silver bridle. Fort Marion,
St. Augustine, Florida.

Smithsonian Institution National
Anthropological Archives. 08517800

ARE AMERICAN INDIANS ESPECIALLY FAST RUNNERS?

Health and physical activities were traditionally extremely important in Native American life. Survival itself depended on the ability to be mobile, vigorous, and strong, and running had numerous traditional purposes among the varied tribes of North and South America. Communication was one of the most important. Runners, sometimes as part of relay systems, carried messages quickly between communities. Running was also an important element of war, trade, and hunting. In some places the activity has long been incorporated into ceremonies and cultural events. For example, each year the Jicarilla Apache people of New Mexico reenact a ceremonial race that, according to traditional belief, occurred long ago between the sun and the moon. Sun and moon had raced to establish appropriate seasons for all the different kinds of plant and animal foods. Today the race is run by unmarried boys of the White Clan, who represent the sun and the animal foods, against the boys of the Red Clan, who represent the moon and the plant foods.

Before European contact, American Indians participated in many other kinds of traditional athletic activities. These included archery, the games of lacrosse and shinny (a precursor to field hockey), wrestling, numerous ball games, arrow toss, pin and ring games, the winter sport of snow snake—which involved skidding long smooth poles along a track of packed snow—canoeing, and kayaking, to name a few. Many of these activities built skills among youth that would be critical in adult life. When communities or tribes gathered, they often held contests that involved running, archery, wrestling, and physical strength.

After the arrival of Europeans it became increasingly difficult

for Native Americans to maintain their traditions. With the advent of boarding schools, however, in the late 1800s, Native Americans were gradually introduced to European American sports and began to participate in football, track and field, baseball, basketball, boxing, and other sports.

In the twentieth century a number of Native Americans excelled in these sports and competed at the highest levels. Probably the most famous Native athlete was Jim Thorpe, a Sac and Fox from Oklahoma. He played collegiate and professional football and baseball, and won gold medals in the pentathlon and decathlon in the 1912 Olympics.

Many other Native American athletes have made their mark in sports history as well. Lewis Tewanima (Hopi) set an American record and won a silver Olympic medal in the ten-thousand-meter run in 1912. In 1964, Tewanima's record was broken by Billy Mills (Oglala Lakota), who won the event at the Tokyo Olympics that year. Several Native American baseball players achieved success at the professional level. Charles Bender (Chippewa) was a pitcher who played in the early 1900s for the Philadelphia Athletics and the Chicago White Sox. He pitched in the World Series and in 1953 was the first Native American elected to the baseball Hall of Fame.

During the early part of the twentieth century, life in the professional leagues could be difficult for Native Americans. Fans and opposing teams commonly hurled epithets and racial slurs at the athletes. Even worse, Native athletes were often paid much less than their non-Native teammates. As times changed and civil rights laws were enacted and enforced, Native Americans began to compete as equals. Today Native athletes participate in many professional and collegiate sports, including hockey and lacrosse.

While Native Americans have enjoyed success in sports, there is a desire among communities and tribes to increase both recreational and competitive athletics among young people especially. School and intramural sports, such as basketball, are hugely popular on western reservations, and many boys' and girls' teams compete in Indian leagues and tournaments. Unfortunately health, educational, and economic disparities make it difficult for Native Americans to get to college and to compete at that level. Numerous national and tribal organizations, however, are working to promote academics and athletics in Native communities and support Native athletes in their efforts to reach higher levels of competition.

Traditional athletic activities are still important in American Indian communities as well, and in some cases are enjoying a revival.

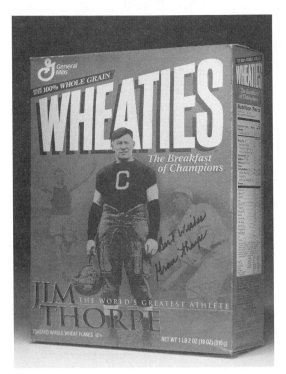

Wheaties cereal box with image of Jim Thorpe (Sac and Fox), autographed by his granddaughter, Grace Thorpe. Gift of James Kincaid Johnson and Peggy Fontenot.

26/4641

The North American Indigenous Games, an organized competition held every four years, offers an opportunity for Native athletes to compete rigorously in sports based on traditional activities. With the current interest in sports and physical activities in tribal communities, the future seems bright for Native athletes.

—EDWIN SCHUPMAN

How Authentic Are Contemporary Movies That Try to Tell Stories From a Native Perspective?

There is no real consensus among critics on the accuracy of fictional movies telling a story from a Native perspective. For some, the mere fact that such movies exist is positive in and of itself, but others take a more critical stance, particularly toward movies written, directed, or produced by Native people. While there have been admirable attempts, such as *Powwow Highway* (1989), by non-Natives to create films from a Native perspective, Native filmmakers bear a much greater responsibility to tell accurate stories that do not build upon existing stereotypes. How they break down false imagery differs from film to film.

The rise of Native filmmaking was inspired by the civil rights movement and the emergence of Native political consciousness. Beginning in 1966, organized attempts to train Native people in the art of filmmaking as well as the rise of independent film and the video format gave many Native filmmakers, for whom the door to commercial success had been closed, a viable outlet for expression. Since then numerous Native film festivals—including the NMAI's biannual Native American Film and Video Festival—have been developed.

The content of Native films is diverse, focusing on political or social issues, culture and history, environmental degradation, and tribal or familial relationships. Native people have produced documentaries for decades, but commercial studios often argue that most American audiences will be unable to relate to a film composed of Native actors telling a Native story. The 1998 film *Smoke Signals* proved the movie moguls wrong. A landmark in film history, *Smoke Signals* was not only written, directed, and coproduced by Native people, but it also achieved modest success among mainstream U.S. audiences. The film, directed

Movie still from *Smoke Signals* (1998),
directed by Chris Eyre (Cheyenne/Arapaho).

© CORBIS/SYGMA.

by Chris Eyre (Cheyenne/Arapaho) and based on a screenplay by Sherman Alexie (Spokane/Coeur d'Alene), consists almost entirely of Native actors speaking from a Native perspective. Critic Amanda J. Cobb has argued that the success of *Smoke Signals* is in its creation of widely accessible yet uniquely Indian characters and its ability to draw upon the geography and residents of the Coeur d'Alene reservation to present a specific tribal experience. At the same time, the film turns politics on its head by allaying with humor the potential guilt of its white, mainstream audience. Director Chris Eyre tries to convey Native concepts of time, relationships, and storytelling to create complex, multilayered characters that contrast sharply with the one-dimensional caricatures of earlier films. The popularity of *Smoke Signals* allowed Eyre's second full-length feature film, *Skins* (2002), to go straight to commercial distribution.

Some Native people, however, feel that *Smoke Signals* is only a small step forward in the portrayal of Native people in film. The dozens of false images depicted on screen for more than a century cannot be discredited by just a few movies, nor will all Native viewers be satisfied just because a Native person is guiding the filmmaking process.

While most people in the early twentieth century learned about American Indians almost exclusively from the movies, the ability to break down the stereotypes the medium helped create is not something one or even a dozen movies by Native filmmakers can be expected to achieve. But that the ranks of Native filmmakers are growing, and that they are continuing to take back the ways in which Native people are portrayed in popular culture is a good start.

—ARWEN NUTTALL

FURTHER READING*

Adovasio, J. M., with Jake Page. *The First Americans: In Pursuit of Archaeology's Greatest Mystery*. New York: Random House, 2002.

Archuleta, Margaret L., Brenda J. Child, and K. Tsianina Lomawaima, eds. *Away from Home: American Indian Boarding School Experiences, 1879–2000*. Phoenix: Heard Museum, 2000.

Belarde-Lewis, Miranda. *Meet Lydia: A Native Girl from Southeast Alaska*. Washington, D.C.: National Museum of the American Indian in association with Council Oak Books, 2004.

Berkhofer, Robert F., Jr. "White Conceptions of Indians." In *History of Indian-White Relations*. Edited by Wilcomb E. Washburn. Vol. 4, *Handbook of North American Indians*, edited by William C. Sturtevant. Washington, D.C.: Smithsonian Institution, 1988.

Blanchard, Kendall. "Traditional Sports, North and South America." In *Encyclopedia of World Sport: From Ancient Times to the Present*, edited by David Levinson and Karen Christenson. Vol. 3. Santa Barbara: ABC-CLIO, 1996.

Bonar, Eulalie. *Woven by the Grandmothers: Nineteenth-Century Navajo Textiles from the National Museum of the American Indian*. Washington, D.C.: National Museum of the American Indian in association with Smithsonian Institution Press, 1996.

Browning, Tara. *Heartbeat of the People: Music and Dance of the Northern Pow-Wow*. Urbana: University of Illinois Press, 2004.

Bruchac, James, and Joseph Bruchac. *Native American Games and Stories*. Golden, Colo.: Fulcrum Publishing, 2000.

Champagne, Duane. *Contemporary Native American Cultural Issues*. Walnut Creek, Calif.: AltaMira Press, 1999.

Closs, Michael P. *Native American Mathematics*. Austin: University of Texas Press, 1989.

Cobb, Amanda J. "This Is What It Means to Say *Smoke Signals*: Native American Cultural Sovereignty." In *Hollywood's Indian: The Portrayal of the Native American in Film*, edited by Peter C. Rollins and John E. O'Connor. Lexington: University Press of Kentucky, 1998.

Code of Federal Regulations. Title 25, Indians. Chapter 1, Bureau of Indian Affairs, Department of the Interior. Part 83, Procedures for establishing that an American Indian group exists as a tribe. Subpart 7, Mandatory criteria for federal acknowledgment. Washington, D.C: National Archives and Records Administration, Office of the Federal Registrar, and Government Printing Office, April 1, 2006. http://www.access.gpo.gov/nara/.

Cook, Noble David. *Born to Die: Disease and New World Conquest, 1492–1650*. New York: Cambridge University Press, 1998.

*For a more comprehensive bibliography, please visit www.AmericanIndian.si.edu/bookshop

Dejong, David H. *Promises of the Past: A History of Indian Education in the United States*. Golden, Colo.: North American Press, 1993.

Deloria, Vine, Jr. *Custer Died for Your Sins: An Indian Manifesto*. Norman: University of Oklahoma Press, 1970.

———. *God Is Red: A Native View of Religion*, 3rd ed. Golden, Colo.: Fulcrum Publishing, 2003.

———. *Red Earth, White Lies: Native Americans and the Myth of Scientific Fact*. New York: Scribner, 1995.

———, ed. *American Indian Policy in the Twentieth Century*. Norman: University of Oklahoma Press, 1985.

Deloria, Vine, Jr., and David E. Wilkins, *Tribes, Treaties, and Constitutional Tribulations*. Austin: University of Texas Press, 1999.

DeMalle, Raymond J., ed. *Plains*. Vol. 13, pts. 1 and 2, *Handbook of North American Indians*, edited by William C. Sturtevant. Washington, D.C.: Smithsonian Institution, 2001.

Densmore, Frances. *Chippewa Customs*. 1929. Reprint, St. Paul: Minnesota Historical Society Press, 1979.

Derounian-Stodola, Kathryn Zabelle, ed. *Women's Indian Captivity Narratives*. New York: Penguin Books, 1998.

Diamond, Jared. *Guns, Germs, and Steel: The Fates of Human Societies*. New York: W. W. Norton, 1999.

Divina, Fernando, and Marlene Divina. *Foods of the Americas*. Washington, D.C.: National Museum of the American Indian in association with Ten Speed Press, 2004.

Drinnon, Richard. *Facing West: The Metaphysics of Indian Hating and Empire Building*. Norman: University of Oklahoma Press, 1997.

Einhorn, Lois J. *The Native American Oral Tradition: Voices of the Spirit and Soul*. Westport, Connecticut: Praeger Publishers, 2000.

Erdoes, Richard. *The Rain Dance People: The Pueblo Indians, Their Past and Present*. New York: Knopf, 1976.

Fleming, Walter C. *The Complete Idiot's Guide to Native American History*. New York: Alpha, 2003.

Frey, Rodney. *The World of the Crow Indians*. Norman: University of Oklahoma Press, 1989.

Gallay, Alan. *The Indian Slave Trade: The Rise of the English Empire in the American South, 1670–1717*. New Haven, Conn.: Yale University Press, 2002.

Garroutte, Eva Marie. *Real Indians: Identity and the Survival of Native America*. Berkeley: University of California Press, 2003.

Goddard, Ives. "Introduction." In *Languages*. Edited by Ives Goddard. Vol. 17, *Handbook of North American Indians*, edited by William C. Sturtevant. Washington, D.C.: Smithsonian Institution, 1997.

Gourse, Leslie. *Native American Courtship and Marriage Traditions*. New York: Hippocrene Books, 1995.

Green, Rayna D. "The Indian in Popular American Culture." In *History of Indian-White Relations*. Edited by Wilcomb E. Washburn. Vol. 4, *Handbook of North American Indians*, edited by William C. Sturtevant. Washington D.C: Smithsonian Institution, 1988.

Greene, Candace, Lakota Winter Counts. National Anthropological Archives, National Museum of Natural History, Smithsonian Institution. http://wintercounts.si.edu.

Harjo, Suzan Shown. "Note to Congress: Stop Shielding 'Indian' Mascots and Start Defending Indian People." *Indian Country Today*, June 9, 2006. www.indiancountry.com.

Heth, Charlotte, ed. *Native American Dance: Ceremonies and Social Traditions*. Washington, D.C: National Museum of the American Indian in association with Fulcrum Publishing, 1992.

Hill, Tom, and Richard W. Hill Sr., eds. *Creation's Journey: Native American Identity and Belief*. Washington, D.C.: National Museum of the American Indian in association with Smithsonian Institution Press, 1994.

Hirschfelder, Arlene, and Paulette Molin. *The Encyclopedia of Native American Religions: An Introduction*. New York: Facts on File, 1992.

Hodge, Frederick Webb. *Handbook of American Indians North of Mexico*. 2 vols. New York: Pageant Books, 1959.

Harvard Project on American Indian Economic Development. *Honoring Nations 2003: Celebrating Excellence in Tribal Government*. Cambridge, Mass.: Harvard Project on American Indian Economic Development, Harvard University, 2004.

Horse Capture, George P. *Powwow*. Cody, Wyo.: Buffalo Bill Historical Center, 1989.

Horse Capture, George P., and Emil Her Many Horses, eds. *A Song for the Horse Nation: Horses in Native American Cultures*. Washington, D.C: National Museum of the American Indian in association with Fulcrum Publishing, 2006.

Hoxie, Frederick E., ed. *Encyclopedia of North American Indians: Native American History, Culture, and Life from Paleo-Indians to the Present*. Boston: Houghton Mifflin, 1996.

Jensen, V. *Totem Pole Carving: Bringing a Log to Life*. Vancouver: Douglas & McIntyre, 2004.

Johansen, Bruce E., and Donald A. Grinde Jr. *The Encyclopedia of Native American Biography: Six Hundred Life Stories of Important People, from Powhatan to Wilma Mankiller*. New York: Da Capo Press, 1998.

Johnson, Tim, ed. *Spirit Capture: Photographs from the National Museum of the American Indian*. Washington, D.C.: National Museum of the American Indian and Smithsonian Institution Press, 1998.

Johnston, Basil. *The Manitous: The Spiritual World of the Ojibway*. New York: Harper-Collins, 1995.

Josephy, Alvin M., Jr. *Five Hundred Nations: An Illustrated History of North American Indians*. New York: Gramercy Books, 1994.

———. *The Indian Heritage of America*. New York: Houghton Mifflin. 1968. Reprint, 1991.

Kaiser, Rudolph. "Chief Seattle's Speech(es): American Origin and European Reception." In *Recovering the World: Essays on Native American Literature*, edited by Brian Swann and Arnold Krupat. Berkeley: University of California Press, 1987.

Kavasch, Barrie. *Native Harvests: Recipes and Botanicals of the American Indian.* New York: Vintage Books, 1979.

Keoke, Emory Dean, and Kay Marie Porterfield, eds. *Encyclopedia of American Indian Contributions to the World.* New York: Facts on File, 2002.

Kidwell, Clara Sue. "Food and Cuisine." In *Encyclopedia of North American Indians: Native American History, Culture, and Life from Paleo-Indians to the Present*, edited by Frederick E. Hoxie. Boston: Houghton Mifflin, 1996.

Kilpatrick, Jacquelyn. *Celluloid Indians: Native Americans and Film.* Lincoln: University of Nebraska Press, 1999.

Krech III, Shepard. *The Ecological Indian: Myth and History.* New York: W. W. Norton, 1999.

Lincoln, Kenneth. *Indi'n Humor: Bicultural Play in Native America.* New York: Oxford University Press, 1993.

Loadman, John. *Tears of the Tree: The Story of Rubber—a Modern Marvel.* New York: Oxford University Press, 2005.

Lyman, Christopher M. *The Vanishing Race and Other Illusions: Photographs of Indians by Edward S. Curtis.* Washington D.C: Smithsonian Institution Press, 1982.

Machamer, Gene. *The Illustrated Native American Profiles.* Mechanicsburg, Pa: Carlisle Press, 1996.

Mann, Charles C. *1491: New Revelations of the Americas before Columbus.* New York: Knopf, 2005.

McLuhan, T. C. *Dream Tracks: The Railroad and the American Indian, 1890–1930.* New York: Harry N. Abrams, 1985.

McMaster, Gerald, and Clifford E. Trafzer, eds. *Native Universe: Voices of Indian America.* Washington, D.C.: National Museum of the American Indian in association with National Geographic Books, 2004.

Mihesuah, Devon A. *American Indians: Stereotypes and Realities.* Atlanta: Clarity Press, 1997.

———. *Cultivating the Rosebuds: The Education of Women at the Cherokee Female Seminary, 1851–1909.* Urbana: University of Illinois Press, 1993.

Moerman, Daniel E. *Native American Ethnobotany.* Portland: Timber Press, 1998.

Moorehead, W. K., and J. E. Kelly. *Cahokia Mounds.* Tuscaloosa: University of Alabama Press, 2000.

Nabokov, Peter. *Indian Running: Native American History and Tradition.* Santa Fe: Ancient City Press, 1981.

Nabokov, Peter, and Robert Easton. *Native American Architecture.* New York: Oxford University Press, 1989.

National Museum of the American Indian. *Listening to Our Ancestors: Native Life along the North Pacific Coast.* Washington, D.C: National Museum of the American Indian in association with National Geographic Books, 2005.

Niethammer, Carolyn. *Daughters of the Earth: The Lives and Legends of American Indian Women.* New York: Simon & Schuster, 1977.

Ohén:ton Kariwahtékwen/Thanksgiving Address: Greetings to the Natural World. Corrales, N.Mex.: Six Nations Indian Museum and Tracking Project, 1993.

Page, Jake. *In the Hands of the Great Spirit: The 20,000-Year History of American Indians.* New York: Free Press, 2003.

Paterek, Josephine. *The Encyclopedia of American Indian Costume.* New York: W. W. Norton, 1994.

Perdue, Theda. "Slavery." In *Encyclopedia of North American Indians: Native American History, Culture, and Life from Paleo-Indians to the Present,* edited by Frederick E. Hoxie. Boston: Houghton Mifflin, 1996.

Pevar, Stephen L. *The Rights of Indians and Tribes: The Basic ACLU Guide to Indian and Tribal Rights.* Carbondale: Southern Illinois University Press, 1992.

Rollins, Peter C., and John E. O'Connor, eds. *Hollywood's Indian: The Portrayal of the Native American in Film.* Lexington: University Press of Kentucky, 1998.

Roscoe, Will. *The Zuni Man-Woman.* Albuquerque: University of New Mexico Press, 1991.

Rose, Cynthia, and Duane Champagne. *Native North American Almanac.* Farmington Hills, Mich.: Thomson Gale/U.X.L, 1994.

Rountree, Helen. *Pocahontas's People: The Powhatan Indians of Virginia through Four Centuries.* Norman: University of Oklahoma Press, 1990.

Sayre, Gordon M., ed. *American Captivity Narratives.* Boston: Houghton Mifflin, 2000.

Scarborough, Vernon L., and David R. Wilcox, eds. *The Mesoamerican Ballgame.* Tucson: University of Arizona Press, 1991.

Secakuku, Susan. *Meet Mindy: A Native Girl from the Southwest.* Washington, D.C.: National Museum of the American Indian in association with Beyond Words Publishing, 2003.

Silver, Shirley, and Wick R. Miller. *American Indian Language: Cultural and Social Contexts.* Tucson: University of Arizona Press, 1997.

Smith, Huston, and Reuben Snake. *One Nation Under God: The Triumph of the Native American Church.* Santa Fe: Clear Light Publishers, 1995.

Standing Bear, Luther. *Land of the Spotted Eagle.* Lincoln: University of Nebraska Press, 1978.

Stewart, Hilary. *Totem Poles.* Seattle: University of Washington Press, 1990.

Stewart, Omer C. *Peyote Religion: A History.* Norman: University of Oklahoma Press, 1987.

Suttles, Wayne, ed. *Northwest Coast.* Vol. 7, *Handbook of North American Indians,* edited by William C. Sturtevant. Washington D.C: Smithsonian Institution, 1990.

Swanton, John R. *Chickasaw Society and Religion.* Lincoln: University of Nebraska Press, 2006.

Szasz, Margaret Connell. *Education and the American Indian: The Road to Self-Determination since 1928.* Albuquerque: University of New Mexico Press, 1999.

Tedlock, Dennis. *Popul Vuh: The Mayan Book of the Dawn of Life and the Glories of Gods and Kings.* New York: Touchstone Books, 1996.

Thornton, Russell. *American Indian Holocaust and Survival: A Population History since 1492*. Norman: University of Oklahoma Press, 1987.

Tiller, Veronica E. Velarde., ed. *Tiller's Guide to Indian Country: Economic Profiles of Indian Reservations*. Albuquerque: BowArrow Publishing, 2005.

Trafzer, Clifford E. *As Long as the Grass Shall Grow and Rivers Flow: A History of Native Americans*. Fort Worth: Harcourt College Publishers, 2000.

Trafzer, Clifford E., Jean A. Keller, and Lorene Sisquoc. *Boarding School Blues: Revisiting American Indian Educational Experiences*. Lincoln: University of Nebraska Press, 2006.

U.S. Department of Health and Human Services. *Trends in Indian Health, 1998–1999*. Rockville, Md.: Indian Health Services, 1999.

Utter, Jack. *American Indians: Answers to Today's Questions*. 2nd ed. Norman: University of Oklahoma Press, 2001.

Viola, Herman J. *After Columbus: The Smithsonian Chronicle of the North American Indians*. Washington, D.C.: Smithsonian Books in association with Orion Books, 1990.

Walker, Willard B. "Native Writing Systems." In *Languages*. Edited by Ives Goddard. Vol. 17, *Handbook of North American Indians*, edited by William C. Sturtevant. Washington, D.C.: Smithsonian Institution, 1997.

Wallis, Velma. *Two Old Women: An Alaskan Legend of Betrayal, Courage and Survival*. Fairbanks: Epicenter Press, 1993.

Washburn, Wilcomb E. "Introduction." In *History of Indian-White Relations*. Edited by Wilcomb E. Washburn. Vol. 4, *Handbook of North American Indians*, edited by William C. Sturtevant. Washington D.C: Smithsonian Institution, 1988.

Weatherford, Jack McIver. *Indian Givers: How the Indians of the Americas Transformed the World*. New York: Ballantine, 1988.

Welburn, Ron. *Roanoke and Wampum: Topics in Native American Heritage and Literature*. New York: Peter Lang Publishing, 2001.

Wilkinson, Charles F. *Blood Struggle: The Rise of Modern Indian Nations*. New York: W. W. Norton, 2005.

Wright, Barton. *Classic Hopi and Zuni Kachina Figures*. Santa Fe: Museum of New Mexico Press, 2006.

———. *Hopi Kachinas: The Complete Guide to Collecting Kachina Dolls*. 1st rev. ed. Flagstaff: Northland Publishing, 2000.

Wright, Ronald. *Stolen Continents: The Americas through Indian Eyes since 1492*. Boston: Houghton Mifflin, 1992.

INDEX

Page numbers in *italics* refer to illustrations.

Quechuan language family, 166
Quechuas, 166, 203, 211
quipus, 180, *180*

racism, 13, 15, 58
rain dances, 107–8
Raleigh, Sir Walter, 103
Raven, 62, 113, 204
ravens, 164, 194
Red Road, The, 212
redskin, as offensive term, 18
religion, 102, 113–14, 117–18, 148, 157, 182
rememberers (*quipu camayacs*), 180
repatriation, of objects and remains,
    144–47
reservations, 4–5, 123–25, 137, 139–40, 186,
    217
    poverty on, 135–36
reserves, 123–25
Rickard, Jolene, 21
rocks, 157–58, 207
Rolfe, John, 38, 104
Rolfe, Thomas, 38
Roman Catholic Church, 114, 198
romances, 192–93, *193*
Romero, Mateo, 17
Roosevelt, Theodore, 64
Roscoe, Will, 197
Round Dance, 209
rubber, 30, 98, 202–3
rubber balls, 25, 98, 202

Sacagawea, 45–46, *46*
sacred songs, 213–14
Sacs, 34
    and Foxes, 220, *221*
salmon, 82, *153*, 155–56, *155*
Sanders, Thomas E., 12
San Juan Pueblo, 4, 117
scalping, 18, 100–101
Schaghticoke Tribe, 122
Schemitzun, 215
Schoolcraft, Henry Rowe, 18
Seattle, Chief, 55–56, *56*
Secakuku, Mindy, 185
Secakuku, Scott, *185*
Seminole, 53, 126, 127
Senate Committee on Indian Affairs, 57,
    190

Senecas, 7, 41, 126
Sequoyah, 170, *170*
Seris, 211
Shakopee Mdewakanton Sioux (Dakota)
    Community, 131, 133–34
shamans, 115–16
Shawnees, 47, *51*, 52
Shoshones, 30, 43, 45–46
    Western, 88
Silverheels, Jay (Harry Smith), 66–68, *67*
singing, 213–14
Sioux, 6, 105, 164, 175
    Shakopee Mdewakanton (Dakota)
        Community, 131, 133–34
    Sisseton Band of Upper, *138*
    Wahpeton Band of Upper, *138*
    Yankton Tribe of, 133–34
    see also Dakotas; Lakotas; Nakotas
Six Nations Powwow, *127*
slavery, 53–54
smallpox, 43–44, 51
Smith, Henry A., 55–56
Smith, John, 38–40
Smithsonian Institution, 196
    see also National Museum of the
        American Indian
smoke signals, 71–72
Smoke Signals, 63, 71, 222–23, *223*
snow, words for, 177–78
socks, 85–86
Soto, Hernando de, 50–51, 100
South America, 2, 5, 9, 25, 50–51, 54, 60,
    75, 102, 103, 124, 159, 166, 202, 203,
    206
    indigenous population of, 120
South Carolina, 54, 126
South Dakota, 46, 58, 133
Southwest, 19, 30, 53–54, 78, 92, 107–8,
    116, 161, 184, 194, 199, 208
sovereignty, 5, 128–29, 136, 148
Spain, 50–51, 60
    colonists from, 2, 6, 27, 31, 54, 103, 161
Spanish Conquest, 80, 98, 169, 207
Spanish language, 2, 5, 166
sports teams, offensive names of, 15–17
squashes, 25, 29, 80–81, 155
squaw, as offensive term, 12–13, 15
Standing Bear, Luther, 154
stereotypes, 69, 100, 223–24